Ridding Your Home of Spiritual Darkness

D0974491

Chuck D. Pierce
and
Rebecca Wagner Sytsema

WAGNER
PUBLICATIONS

Ridding Your Home of Spiritual Darkness
Copyright © 2000
by Chuck D. Pierce and Rebecca Wagner Sytsema
ISBN 1-58502-008-7

Published by
Wagner Publications
11005 N. Highway 83
Colorado Springs, CO 80921
www.wagnerpublications.org

Cover design by
Erin Mathis
emdesign Studio
1035 Tehama Avenue
Menlo Park, CA 94025
www.emdesignstudio.com

7 8 9 10   06 05 04

TABLE OF CONTENTS

1. SPIRITUAL LIFE, LIBERTY, AND FREEDOM   5

2. BECOMING AWARE OF SPIRITUAL DARKNESS   11

3. THE JEWELRY BOX   17

4. SPIRITUAL DISCERNMENT   25

5. A DEMONIC FOOTHOLD IN THE LAND   33

6. OVERTHROWING GENERATIONAL CURSES   43

7. PROTECTING OUR CHILDREN FROM SPIRITUAL DARKNESS   51

8. TEN STEPS TO RIDDING YOUR HOME OF SPIRITUAL DARKNESS   61

APPENDIX ONE: RECOMMENDED READING   70

APPENDIX TWO: PRAYER OF RELEASE FOR FREEMASONS AND THEIR DESCENDANTS   72

CHAPTER ONE

SPIRITUAL LIFE, LIBERTY, AND FREEDOM

The loud crash of thunder jerked Cathy (not her real name) from her troubled thoughts. Pulling the curtain aside, she peered out at the ominous clouds that had suddenly filled the Texas sky. The turbulent weather only served as a dark reminder of Cathy's own life as a fresh wave of the all-too-familiar depression seemed to overcome her once again. She could barely move under the weight of her own cloud that had nothing to do with the summer afternoon's storm.

Cathy, who had been our friend for some time, often suffered from bouts of deep, overwhelming depression. Despite counseling and prayer, we had never discovered the source of her constant gloom. As I was visiting with her one day, she asked me about a Greek statue that had been given to her by her former husband. She wondered if perhaps that statue had something to do with her depression. I agreed that the statue had to go, but I knew deep within my spirit that it was not linked with her suffering. Even so, I knew that something in her house was not right. I knew that some *thing* was connected to the dark shadow that hung over her emotions. I began walking through the house praying, "Lord, show me any thing in this home which is representing Cathy's depression."

We looked at many antiques she had collected through the years. While antiques are often laden with demonic oppression, I knew that none of these objects was the problem. Then the Lord led me over to a glass bookcase. I knew in my spirit that there was something in that bookcase that needed to go. I reached up to the top shelf and pulled out a book that turned out to be a handbook for 32nd degree Masons. Cathy had no idea where the book came from, or that it was in her home. Immediately I knew that the book had to be destroyed, so we built a fire and burned it.

That act was a turning point in Cathy's life. It set in motion a chain of events which led to a Masonic curse being broken in her bloodline. As that curse was broken, the gripping, overwhelming depression that had been Cathy's constant companion completely let go of her mind, and she has walked in freedom ever since. Finding that book was a key to exposing Satan's stronghold over her emotions. Destroying the book was an act of obedience that led to the eventual dismantling of that stronghold and to the liberty that Cathy enjoys today.

What happened to Cathy? How did I know what object needed to go? Were any demonic forces attached to the book? What did Cathy's bloodline have to do with her suffering? We hope to offer answers to these and many other questions concerning how demonic forces work within our own homes. It is our prayer that this book will help you do any spiritual housecleaning you may need to do in order to rid your home of spiritual darkness.

Understanding Spiritual Life

The thief does not come except to steal, and to kill, and to destroy. I have come that they may have life, and that they may have it more abundantly (John 10:10).

Jesus' words in John 10:10 are not only a great comfort to His followers, but a profound key to understanding the war in which we as Christians find ourselves. There is a thief who has come to steal, kill, and destroy. He is the enemy of our souls, and it is important that we are wise to his schemes. The real issue in understanding how Satan works to bring death is to have an understanding of spiritual life. If we do not understand spiritual life, we will not be able to see where death has gained access and established itself in our homes.

The "life" that Jesus has come to give us is translated from the Greek word *zoe* which means to be possessed of vitality; to have life active and vigorous; to be devoted to God; to be blessed; to be among the living (not lifeless or dead); to enjoy real life, true life worthy of the name; to pass life on to others; to be fresh, strong, efficient, active, powerful; to be endless in the kingdom of God.[1] Furthermore, Jesus tells us that He has come to give us this rich existence more abundantly; which means excessive, overflowing, surplus, over and above, more than enough, profuse, extraordinary, more than sufficient, superior, more remarkable, more excellent.[2]

The abundant life that Christ brings is not a promise of a fairy tale story where, as we are living happily ever after, we find continual joy in our perfect life. In fact, the Bible clearly states that opposite is true: "In the world you will have tribulation" (John 16:33). However, that verse goes on to say, "but be of good cheer, I have overcome the world." The Apostle Paul takes it one step further by saying, "we also glory in tribulations, knowing that tribulation produces perseverance; and perseverance, character; and character, hope" (Rom. 5:3-4).

Because of our covenant relationship with God, even in times of tribulation, suffering, or loss, we have the promise of abundant, *zoe* life. According to Isaiah 61, Jesus is anointed to heal the brokenhearted, proclaim liberty to the captives, give beauty for ashes, the oil of joy for mourning, and a garment of praise for the spirit of heaviness. Such promises are the heritage of God's children. Our joy does not come from a perfect, pain-free life, but rather from a peace that passes understanding—from an intimate relationship with the author of *zoe* life.

Liberty and Freedom

Part of the *zoe* life that we as Christians enjoy is liberty and free-dom. Liberty is defined as freedom from control, interference, obligation, restriction, external or foreign rule. Freedom is de-fined as immunity, exemption, and the power to enjoy all the privileges or special rights of citizenship. Jesus lived, died, and rose again to bring us liberty from the bondages of death, hell, and the grave—that is, freedom from control, interference, obli-gation, restriction, or the rule of Satan. Jesus' shed blood gives us freedom to come before God with immunity and exemption from sin, and gives us the power to enjoy all the privileges and special rights of heavenly citizenship.

The Indwelling and Empowering Work of the Holy Spirit

The very basis of experiencing *zoe* life is the ministry of the Holy Spirit to each and every one of us. As my own pastor for many years, Robert Heidler, writes in his book, *Experiencing the Spirit*, "The indwelling Spirit is the Spirit of Jesus living in the hearts of His people, sent to give them new hope, new love, new peace, new joy, and new direction. This ministry is foundational to ev-erything else in the Christian life. Through the indwelling Spirit we are *sealed* in Christ and given an inner assurance that we be-long to Him (see 2 Cor. 1:22)...

"Why would the Spirit of God want to live inside people like you and me? He lives in our hearts to enable us to live life on a new level. He is working to *change* us from the inside out, so that we may become more like Jesus."[3]

Every Christian, at the time they accepted Christ, received the indwelling of the Holy Spirit. We know this is so because we are called the "temple of the Holy Spirit" (1 Cor. 6:19). It comes with Christianity. But, as Heidler goes on to point out, being *empowered* by the Holy Spirit is another matter. "The *indwelling* ministry of the Spirit is automatic...He came and took up residence within your heart at the moment of your salvation. In contrast, the *empowering* of the Spirit is seldom automatic, usually coming instead in response to prayer."[4] Empowering of the Spirit is just as much a part of *zoe* life as indwelling of the Spirit. Why is this important to the subject at hand, which is ridding your home of spiritual darkness? It is because we need the empowering work of the Spirit in order to wage warfare against the enemy. No demonic force will ever comply with our commands to be gone without spiritual power backing us up. The empowering work of the Spirit gives us the authority we need to evict demons from our homes and lives.

Cooperating With the Holy Spirit

Because the empowering of the Holy Spirit is not automatic, but rather something which we must pursue, we need to learn ways to cooperate with what the Holy Spirit is longing to do. Here is a list of eight principles for living a life prepared to receive empowerment:

1. Meditation on the Word of God.
2. Prayer.
3. Fasting.
4. Giving.
5. Repentance.
6. Worship.
7. Work.
8. Rest.

In the book, *Possessing Your Inheritance* (Renew), we go into detail on each of these points. For now, however, it is enough that we are aware of these principles and understand that as we follow them, we are allowing the Holy Spirit to empower us with what we need to defeat the enemy within our homes.

Notes

[1] James Strong, *The New Strong's Exhaustive Concordance of the Bible* (Nashville, TN: Thomas Nelson Publisher, 1990). ref. 2198 and 2222.

[2] Ibid, ref. 4053.

[3] Robert Heidler, *Experiencing the Spirit*, (Ventura, CA: Renew Books, 1998), pp. 51, 54.

[4] Ibid. p. 88.

CHAPTER TWO

BECOMING AWARE OF SPIRITUAL DARKNESS

If we are to supposed to be partakers of *zoe* life and live in the liberty and freedom just described, why do so many Christians suffer from oppression (like Cathy), fear, low self image, depression, uncontrollable sin patterns, and other bondages that produce death rather than life?

The two main reasons why Christians do not enjoy the *zoe* life that God has promised are: 1. sin and 2. Satan. We will deal more with the issues of sin, both personal and generational, in later chapters. Here, however, let's take a look at Satan and the forces he uses to steal the fullness from our lives.

As C. Peter Wagner states in his book, *Warfare Prayer*, "Satan's central task and desire is to prevent God from being glorified. Whenever God is not glorified in a person's life, in a church, in a city, or in the world as a whole, Satan has to that degree accomplished his objective...Satan's primary objective is to prevent God from being glorified by keeping lost people from being saved... Satan's secondary objective is to make human beings and human society as miserable as possible in this present life."[1]

How is it that Satan manages to make so many of us as miserable as he possibly can in this present life? He delegates. At the enemy's disposal is a vast demonic host assigned to see that Christians never reach their full potential while on earth. In so doing, they have not only succeeded in causing us distress and grief, but they have also succeeded in keeping us from fulfilling the destiny that God has for us in this lifetime. God has a purpose, a great destiny for each and every one of us. This destiny is not only meant to cause us to live *zoe* life, but is designed to advance the Kingdom of God on earth. Getting us off course is, therefore, well worth Satan's effort. He can steal *zoe* life from us and thwart God's purpose for our lives at the same time.

Clever Disguises

While there are many ways that demonic forces can oppress God's people, this book is written to help us discover how these forces gain a foothold within our own homes. We must first understand that demons have many clever disguises they use to keep us ignorant of their work in our lives. As Noel and Phyl Gibson say in *Evicting Demonic Intruders*, "Demons cover their existence by deception, so that people concentrate on what they see, or how they feel, and overlook spiritual causes."[2] The Gibsons go on to list four reasons why Christians may be unaware of demonic activity:

1. Fear of demons causes people to deny their existence.
2. Lack of spiritual discernment.
3. Most modern preaching and teaching avoid the subject of demonic activity.
4. First century faith has largely been replaced by twentieth century rationalism.[3]

To this list I would add,

5. Our Western mindset keeps us from validating that which cannot be explained through scientific study.

As believers we must come to an understanding that there is often an invisible, spiritual force behind a visible object. This is one way that demons operate. Second Corinthians 4:18 says, "We do not look at the things which are seen, but at the things which are not seen. For the things which are seen are temporary, but the things which are not seen are eternal." Here Paul implies that there is more we need to be aware of than that which we can perceive with our five natural senses.

Demons are masters of disguise. They can inhabit people, objects, portions of land, or whole territories, depending on their purpose. They do not care *what* they inhabit, as long as they can accomplish their assigned objectives. They can gain access through sin, trauma, victimization, witchcraft, occult practices, or cursing. While we do not want to become fascinated with demons, we must be aware of what they are and how they operate in order to keep our own homes free of spiritual darkness.

Haunted Houses?

When my coauthor, Rebecca Sytsema, first met her husband, Jack, he asked her to come over to the apartment he was renting from the seminary he attended in order to pray. He reported that there was always a heavy, oppressive feeling inside the apartment. He didn't like being there at all. He knew the problem was spiritual and needed prayer.

When they arrived at the apartment, Jack gave Rebecca a quick tour and they began praying. An ominous feeling descended on them both. It was as if a dark shroud draped itself over the room. Suddenly, the microwave (which had not been in use) began beeping. The answering machine began making strange noises, rewinding itself and playing old, erased messages. The lights began to flicker on and off—all within a matter of seconds, and all without explanation. Jack and Rebecca began praying harder!

Within a few minutes, a neighbor (who was also a seminary student), stormed down the stairs, began pounding on the door, and yelled a string of obscenities at Jack for causing the mysterious electrical fluctuations that were now apparently affecting the whole building. There had been no history of electrical problems there, and certainly no way for that man to know that anything was going on in Jack's apartment. Without a doubt, Jack and Rebecca had stirred up demonic forces that would have preferred to remain incognito.

In the Name of Jesus, Jack took authority as the legal tenant of that apartment and commanded those spirits to leave. By the leading of the Holy Spirit, he repented for any past sins that had been committed there. He anointed the doors and windows with oil and consecrated the apartment to the Lord. By the time they were done praying, great peace filled his home. Jack reported that he got his first good night's sleep since moving in several months earlier. A few weeks later Jack sensed that the spirits were trying to regain residence. He and two other friends prayed through the apartment once again, and he had no further spiritual trouble for the remaining time he lived in that apartment.

Was the apartment "haunted"? In a manner of speaking the answer is yes. It was not haunted by ghosts of human beings, but rather by demonic forces whose job was to cloud the air with oppressive darkness. And what better place to set up camp than in seminary housing where tomorrow's Christian leaders are supposed to receive training for ministry?

Does My Home Need Prayer?

There is always a great deal of benefit in praying through a home for the purpose of consecrating or setting it apart for the Lord. By doing this, you may or may not encounter spiritual darkness that needs to be dealt with. But there are indicators as to whether or not a home needs to be cleansed of spiritual darkness. Following is a list which was taken from Eddie Smith's booklet, *Spiritual Housecleaning*, that might indicate symptoms of a "spiritually polluted atmosphere" which requires spiritual cleansing:

· Ongoing illness
· Continual bad dreams and nightmares
· Insomnia
· Behavioral problems
· Relational problems; continual fighting and arguing
· No peace
· Restless, disturbed children
· Unexplained illnesses or bondage
· "Ghosts" or demonic apparitions (to which children are particularly susceptible)
· Poltergeists (the movement of physical objects by demons)
· Foul, unexplainable odors
· Atmospheric heaviness making it hard to breathe
· Continual nausea and headaches[4]

If you are experiencing any of these things on an ongoing basis, ask the Lord to reveal any spiritual darkness that may be in your home. Remember that Jesus has given us authority over these beings and that He is far greater than any force that might come against you. There is no need to fear. Becoming aware of the demonic and how it may be affecting you is the first step to ridding your home of spiritual darkness!

Notes

[1] C. Peter Wagner, *Warfare Prayer* (Ventura, CA: Regal Books, 1992), p. 61.
[2] Noel and Phyl Gibson, *Evicting Demonic Intruders* (Ventura, CA: Renew Books, 1993), p. 47.
[3] Ibid, pp. 48-49.
[4] Eddie Smith, *Spiritual Housecleaning* (Houston, TX: SpiriTruth Publishing Co., 1997) p. 9.

CHAPTER THREE

THE JEWELRY BOX

M y wife had to be crazy! What other explanation could there be for wanting to destroy a beautiful—and valuable—jewelry box? There was nothing wrong with that box. How ridiculous! How wasteful!

Such were my thoughts on the day my wife, Pam, came home from a prayer meeting and told me that her jewelry box had to go. Little did I know that the Lord would use that jewelry box to deliver me from a covetous, greedy spirit, *and* teach me the truth about demonic forces inhabiting objects at the same time.

It happened several years ago. Pam was enjoying a spiritual revival in her life. During that time, she and six other ladies decided to meet together for seven weeks to pray for their husbands in order to see them come into a deeper spiritual walk and to experience renewal in their own lives. In the sixth week of their prayer time, a friend, who was a missionary to China, came to the prayer meeting. She began to discuss with them how demonic forces could inhabit objects in order to bring spiritual darkness into a home. Having lived in China, this missionary had a different approach to spiritual issues than those of us with a Western mindset. Her perspective made sense to Pam.

When Pam came home after that meeting she started telling me what the missionary shared with them. She told me that she could not stop thinking about a large, beautiful jewelry box that her father had brought her from Thailand. The jewelry box was decorated with dragons, pagodas, and Buddhas—all kinds of images that she knew did not bring glory to God. The more she thought about it, the more she felt the box had to go.

I thought she was totally off the wall! I was aware of spiritual darkness, but had no idea that demons could attach themselves to objects. So I told her that first of all, she was crazy for thinking that anything spiritual was linked to that jewelry box. And second of all, I reminded her that the box was a gift and that it was worth a lot of money. Why would we want to destroy a valuable object? My wife immediately submitted to me and did not mention it any more.

Three weeks later we were in some friends' home attending a prayer meeting. During that meeting the Spirit of God spoke to me and said, "You have caused your wife to rebel against My will for her life, and I hold you accountable!" Immediately I knew the Lord was talking about the jewelry box. He had revealed to Pam that she needed to destroy it and I stopped her from obeying Him! At that moment a deep fear of the Lord came over me. I knew that as soon as we got home I had to take responsibility for what I had done and burn that jewelry box myself.

When we got home, I immediately set a fire in the fireplace. I did not know exactly what I was doing, but I knew I had to do it. When I placed the jewelry box in the fireplace, a strange, eerie wind began to blow and stir all around the living room. The wind was not coming from outside. Something was generating it from within our home! The inexplicable wind blew so hard that it knocked a lamp clear off of the wall.

Not knowing exactly what I was dealing with, I became frightened.

At that time, I knew of a woman in our church who understood spiritual things. So I called her, told her what was going on, and asked her what to do. She began to pray for me over the phone. She told me to read some Scriptures and command any evil presence linked with that jewelry box to leave our home. When I did so the Lord spoke to me and said, "I am delivering you from covetousness and the love of money!"

Once I was liberated from that particular demonic force in my life, it was as if my eyes were opened to many issues within our home that were linked with other evil forces. Freedom began to come to us in incredible ways. Not only freedom, but spiritual revelation.

What Did the Jewelry Box Represent?

So, what did the jewelry box have to do with covetousness and the love of money? At first it had nothing to do with it. The jewelry box had images that were not glorifying to God in the form of dragons, pagodas and Buddhas. They were carven images of gods and creatures worshiped in the Thai culture. That was why the Holy Spirit convicted Pam to get rid of it.

When I stood in the way of ridding our home of unclean images on the basis of the object's monetary value, my own covetousness and greed, and the demonic forces that had been in my family concerning those issues, became linked with the jewelry box. In other words, it was simply a matter of my unwillingness to obey God and destroy something of value, so that object became a symbol of an evil force in my life. When the fear of the Lord came on me and I chose to destroy the box, no matter what its value, that act broke the back of a demonically inspired love of money that had been passed down to me from my father (we will get into this issue of generational iniquity in Chapter Six). God was able to deliver my home of an unclean object, *and* deliver me of a covetous spirit at the same time.

Taking a Look at What We Own

The jewelry box brings up two distinct instances of objects that need to be dispatched in order to rid our home of spiritual darkness—1. objects that do not bring glory to God, and 2. objects that represent demonic strongholds in our own lives. Let's look at each one of these instances.

Objects That Do Not Bring Glory to God

Once we become aware of spiritual darkness, we can begin looking around in our homes and see what we own that does not bring glory to God. What we mean by this phrase is something that, by its very nature, can attract or be inhabited by darkness. Here are five categories of such objects:

1. "Foreign Gods." "You shall not make for yourself any carved image— any likeness of anything that is in heaven above, or that is in the earth beneath, or that is in the water under the earth;" (Deut. 5:8). In this, the second of the ten commandments, a "carved image" refers to any tangible object that represents an idol, god, or demonic figure. Not only is this a welcome mat for demonic activity, God also hates it. Though it may be out of ignorance, it is surprising to realize how many Christians have such items in their homes.

These objects may include Buddhas (like those on the jewelry box); Hindu images; fertility gods or goddesses (or any type of god or goddess); Egyptian images; Greek gods; gargoyles; kachina dolls, totem poles, or any other native figure that depicts or glorifies a "spirit" or demonic being; evil depictions of creatures such as lions, dogs, dragons, cats, or any other creature made with demonic distortions; or any other image of any person, idol, god, or demonic figure which is considered an object of worship or spiritual power in any culture of the world. Many of these types of artifacts are collected as souvenirs on trips without an understanding of their significance—much like the jewelry box which came from Thailand.

A commonly seen item in the United States that falls into this category is images of the Virgin Mary, who is often worshiped by many as an equal to Jesus. C. Peter Wagner calls the worship of Mary a "deceptive adaptation" by the Queen of Heaven, a high-ranking demonic principality, to gain worship that should belong to God. In fact, this counterfeit Mary is often referred to as the Queen of Heaven.[1] By including this, I am not suggesting that we discard our nativity scenes at Christmas. But statues, paintings, and other images depicting Mary as the Queen of Heaven (especially when the image includes a royal crown or a crescent moon) exalts her to the point of a goddess with real spiritual power, rather than the blessed young woman whom God chose to bear Jesus.

2. False Religions. Objects or materials related to false religions such as Mormonism, Islam, Jehovah's Witnesses, Hinduism, eastern religions, Christian Science, native religions, Baha'i, and so forth need to be carefully evaluated. This would include instruction books on Yoga, transcendental meditation, mantras, and so forth.

3. Occult Objects. Anything related to the occult must be destroyed completely. These objects would include Ouija boards; good luck charms; amulets; astrology items including horoscopes; tarot cards; crystals; fetishes; water witching sticks; voodoo dolls; pagan symbols; dream catchers; crystal balls; any item used in rituals such as masks, rain sticks, native drums; pyramids and obelisks; any item obtained from occult or voodoo shops; any item related to black magic, fortune telling, palmistry, demon worship, spirit guides, witchcraft, Satanism or New Age. None of these or any other such items should have any place in the Christian home.

4. Secret Society Objects. Remember the story in Chapter One about Cathy and the handbook for 32nd degree Masons? That book was connected to her depression. Secret societies such as Freemasonry, Shriners, Eastern Star, Job's Daughters, Oddfellows, Elks, Amaranth, De Molay, Rainbow Girls, or Daughters of the Nile often require their members to take oaths and go through initiation rituals that are completely contrary to God's Word, including pledging allegiance to various deities. Because that is the case, demons can easily attach themselves to items representing those societies such as books, rings, aprons, regalia, and memorabilia. Because such items are often passed down through family lines, there is a generational issue that must be dealt with. More about that in Chapter Six.

5. Other Objects. Our homes may be filled with other items that do not bring glory to God and may attract demonic activity. These would include games such as Dungeons and Dragons or Masters of the Universe, in addition to a myriad of demonic or violent video games; books and magazines devoted to fantasy; comic books, posters, movies, or music with demonic, violent, or sexual themes; pornography; illegal drugs; sensual art, books, or "toys"; or a number of other things that are demonic, illegal, immoral, or contrary to God's Word.

By allowing any of these types of things into our homes we give the enemy a legal right to invade our lives in ways that he would otherwise not have. As Cindy Jacobs would say, we have holes in our armor. In order to bring clarity in the process of deciding what might need to go, C. Peter Wagner encourages us to ask the following questions:

· Might this open me to direct demonic influence?
· Does this give any appearance of evil?
· Does this glorify God?[2]

Objects That Represent Demonic Strongholds

Objects that we may possess, although not wrong in themselves, often represent a demonic stronghold in our lives. The jewelry box was just that kind of item in my life. It did have images on it that needed to be cleansed from my house. But even if it didn't, my unwillingness to give it up due to its value shows a much deeper problem that was, in fact, a demonic stronghold of covetousness and the love of money.

The love of money is a big issue, especially in American society. It is the only sin of the flesh (listed in 1 Cor. 5) that is "hard-core idolatry," a term coined by C. Peter Wagner. Referring to Luke 16:13, "You cannot serve both God and Money," Wagner states, "covetousness is allegiance to a false god named Mammon...It is correct to capitalize 'Money' or 'Mammon' because it is a proper name. Mammon is a person, not a thing or an urge or an attitude...When Jesus mentioned Mammon, it was in the context of not being able to serve two masters. Serving any supernatural master in the demonic world, like Mammon, is hard-core idolatry."[3] That was the allegiance that the jewelry box came to represent in my life. When I chose to obey God and get rid of the jewelry box, the demonic force of Mammon lost its grip in my life, and I was delivered.

While covetousness may be the only sin of the flesh that is hard-core idolatry, it is not the only thing that may represent a demonic stronghold in our lives. Take, for example, lust. Perhaps there is something in your home from a past romantic relationship (maybe a gift or some old love letters or hidden photos) and one or both of you is now married to another person. A demonic stronghold of lust or of inappropriate love could easily attach itself to that item. Destroying whatever it is will help you overcome the enemy's grip in that area of your life. It will help you leave the past behind and move forward in God's destiny for you and your family.

Knowing what might represent a demonic stronghold in your life, or what objects are not bringing glory to God, often takes spiritual discernment. In the following chapter we will look at what discernment is and how to use it to rid our homes of spiritual darkness.

Notes

[1] C. Peter Wagner, *Confronting the Queen of Heaven* (Colorado Springs, CO: Wagner Publications, 1998), pp. 31-34.

[2] C. Peter Wagner, *Breaking Strongholds in Your City* (Ventura, CA: Regal Books, 1993), p. 65.

[3] C. Peter Wagner, *Hard-Core Idolatry: Facing the Facts* (Colorado Springs, CO: Wagner Publications, 1999), p. 17.

CHAPTER FOUR

SPIRITUAL DISCERNMENT

"**H**ow do we know when we've prayed enough?" she asked me. The woman and her husband sat across from me describing their situation in some detail. There was a piece of property that they owned. They regularly prayed over it hoping to one day plant a church there. But they knew that something was wrong.

"Every time we set foot on that property, the hair on my arms stands up! We've prayed and prayed. How do we know when we've prayed enough?"

"It's very simple," I told her, "pray until the hair on your arms goes down!"

What Is Spiritual Discernment?

"Spiritual discernment is the grace to see into the unseen. It is a gift *of the Spirit* to perceive what is *in the spirit*. Its purpose is to see into the nature of that which is veiled."[1] This quote from Francis Frangipane is helpful in understanding what discernment is. It is something that we know by seeing with our spiritual eyes rather than with our physical eyes.

Gary Kinnaman defines it this way, "There are three kinds of spirits: evil spirits, human spirits, and heavenly spirits, including angels and the Spirit of God. The discerning of spirits is the ability to identify the kind of spirit that is the driving force behind a particular event, circumstance or thought. If it is determined that the spirit is an evil one, the discerning of spirits operating with precision can also identify the specific kind of evil spirit."[2]

There are some in the Body of Christ who have a gift of discernment. Those with a developed, mature gift are able to discern the spiritual atmosphere of a place or a person more often and with more accuracy than most Christians. But the ability to discern spirits is not limited to those with "the gift." God can speak to any Christian through the Holy Spirit and give spiritual insight into any given situation. Spiritual discernment may seem like a complicated or difficult thing, but the fact is that discernment can be as simple as praying until the hair on your arms goes down. It's a matter of learning how to use the discernment God gives.

A Lamp Unto My Feet

So, how do we learn to have spiritual discernment? Discernment comes through knowing God. There are two main keys to knowing God, which are God's Word and hearing by the spirit through prayer (see Heb. 5:14). They are both important factors to spiritual discernment.

Psalm 119 says, "Through Your precepts I get understanding; therefore I hate every false way. Your word is a lamp to my feet and a light to my path" (vv. 104-105). As we read and digest the Word of God, we develop important spiritual principles within us. Those principles help illuminate the path that God has for us—they act as a lamp unto our feet. For instance, by knowing the Word of God, we understand that we are not to have any carved images of idols in our homes, as we explained in the last chapter. That understanding helps us become sensitive to carved images of idols all around us, whether in our homes, places of work, or whereever we may be.

I have developed a real aversion to any image of idols, false gods, or the demonic because I know how much God hates them. Just as Psalm 119 says, I gained understanding about such images through God's precept (His Word). That understanding helped me become aware of these kinds of images all around me. That understanding has also helped me set a rule about what I will not own, namely images of idols. In that way, God's Word has become a lamp unto my feet. From knowing God's Word, we can look at objects within our homes and see what does not line up with the Bible. That is a part of discernment.

Hearing God

There are certain things we must discern, however, that are not as apparent as the image of an idol. They are spiritual issues and must be discerned spiritually. We must hear from God in order to know what it going on. The key to hearing God is prayer— two-way communication when you speak to Him and He speaks to you.

Hearing the voice of God is not as difficult as some might think. I have found that many of God's people are hearing Him, but have not perceived it as His voice. To perceive means to take hold of, feel, comprehend, grasp mentally, recognize, observe, or become aware of something. We must learn to perceive God's voice and the prompting of the Holy Spirit.

Some ways that God may speak to us include spiritual dreams (dreams that are unusually vivid and detailed and stick in our spirit), visions, visitations, receiving a prophetic word, conversation with a friend that brings revelation, through a message we've heard, or through a feeling—like the woman whose hair stood up on her arms. When we hear from God, we suddenly know that we know something. There is a revelation that takes place in our spirits. Our challenge is to sharpen our spiritual ears to hear God, and to not write off what we hear as mere imagination. God *wants* to communicate with us. We must believe that.

Furthermore, God does not want us to be ignorant of how the enemy is trying to ensnare us. He wants to give us the discernment we need to rid our homes of spiritual darkness.

Spiritual Boundaries

When we have discerned something that we believe is from the Lord, we must allow the Lord to show us what to do with that discernment. This became apparent in my own life not long after the jewelry box incident. From that time on the Lord began to open my eyes to other objects in my home that were linked with demonic forces. My discernment was getting sharper all the time.

One day I was walking by our fireplace and saw a large ceramic cat that I had purchased some time before. It was a beautiful object with piercing blue eyes. The cat was worth a lot of money, but money was no longer an issue since my deliverance from the love of money when I destroyed the jewelry box. As I looked at the cat, I immediately discerned that witchcraft was linked to it. I then remembered that, out of my ignorance, I had purchased the cat in a shop filled with objects used in voodoo rituals while I was on a business trip in New Orleans. I began to see that this cat was linked with spiritism in my bloodline. That was why I was drawn into the voodoo shop in the first place and felt compelled to buy the cat (more about this phenomenon in Chapter Six). I knew the cat had to go. Because it was ceramic, I knew that it would not burn as the jewelry box did. Nonetheless, I passed it through the fire (according to Deut. 7:5), and then smashed it.

In my zeal I began to look around the house for other such

objects. I found many ceramic cats that my wife had collected through the years. Because of spiritual immaturity, I assumed that if the cat I bought was evil then all the other cats were also evil, so I smashed them, too. When she came home later that day, she asked what had happened to her cats. I explained to her what I had done. She just looked at me and said, "There was nothing wrong with my cats. It was *your* cat that had the problem. You have a choice. You can either replace the cats yourself or give me money to buy new ones."

She was absolutely right. My good discernment had run amuck! The problem was not with ceramic cats in general, but with one particular ceramic cat that I had ignorantly purchased in a voodoo shop. I did not heed the spiritual boundaries that should have been obvious, and as a result, I got in a lot of trouble with my wife!

Spiritual Authority

Spiritual boundaries are linked with authority. Each of us is given a sphere of authority in which we are free to operate (see 2 Cor. 10:13). When we get beyond that sphere of authority we run into real problems. Take the cats, for example. Even if there had been demons attached to my wife's ceramic cats, I did not have the authority to destroy them without her permission because they simply did not belong to me.

I have know many people who, upon learning the principles outlined in this book, have made major mistakes because they did not understand their spiritual authority. Armed with discernment and the Name of Jesus, they have felt they can rid the world of demonic forces. That is just not so. We may begin to discern all kinds of problems, but we must understand that we are not free to deal with every problem we see—nor would it be wise.

If you visit your mother's house, for example, and see that she has a statue of Buddha, but she is unwilling to get rid of it, you do not have the right, either legally or spiritually, to take her statue. It is beyond your spiritual authority. What you can do is pray and ask the Lord to reveal these principles to her. Maybe she would be willing to read this book. There may be other things you can do to help her understand, but taking what is not yours definitely crosses the line of authority, not to mention breaking one of the Ten Commandments in the process. Any spirit attached to that statue can actually gain greater power through the sin of stealing.

If your mother, on the other hand, asked you to get rid of the statue and pray for her, then she has given you the authority not only to destroy the statue, but to command any spirits attached to that statue to leave. In this case, she has extended spiritual authority for you to act on her behalf, and you are free to deal with the situation.

Ask the Lord to show you what your sphere of authority is before moving out in presumption and, thereby, making things worse than they were before!

A Gargoyle in the Attic

I am reminded of a good example of spiritual discernment at work. Some years ago I was asked to pray over a building owned by some friends. Their business was located on the bottom floor, and some apartments occupied the top. The building had been plagued with continual problems including flooding. My friends had come to believe that there was a spiritual problem, so they called me. When I entered the building, I immediately knew something was very wrong. The evil was so strong that I couldn't breathe! Through discernment I knew that there was some object within the building that had demonic forces attached to it, and I knew it was somewhere above us.

Because my friends trusted my discernment, they spent $30,000 to tear out the ceiling in order to see what might be there. They found nothing. I knew that, despite their great efforts, something had been missed. Some months later, as they were renovating the building and having electrical work done, they discovered a cement gargoyle hidden in one corner of the attic. I knew that was what we had been looking for! The Lord revealed that the gargoyle had been planted there as a fetish in order to curse the building. We destroyed the gargoyle and prayed through the building, dedicating it to the Lord. Since that time my friends have not encountered any trouble with the building.

Notes

[1] Francis Frangipane, *Discerning of Spirits*, (Cedar Rapids, IA: Arrow Publications, 1991), p. 6.
[2] Gary D. Kinnaman, *Overcoming the Dominion of Darkness*, (Old Tappan, NJ: Chosen Books, 1990), pp.133-134.

CHAPTER FIVE

A DEMONIC FOOTHOLD
IN THE LAND

Elaine awakened suddenly to the anguished screams of her son. "Not again!" she thought to herself as she pulled on her bathrobe and wearily shuffled down the hall to Joey's room. She pushed the door open to find the familiar sight of her three-year-old sobbing on his bed. She dropped onto the bed and, gathering the small boy into her arms, stroked his head which was soaked with tears and sweat.

"It's okay, Joey," she whispered in his ear. "Mommy's here. No one will hurt you." She began to rock him back and forth, as she had so many nights before trying to calm him down. A full hour later Elaine finally crawled back into her own bed, but she could not fall back asleep wondering why her son had not slept one full night since they moved into this house almost six months earlier. He had slept well before, but something here was different.

Enough was enough. The next day Elaine called Joan, the pastor's wife, for counsel and prayer. Joan suggested that perhaps they needed to pray through Joey's room, and agreed to come over that afternoon. As the women began praying,

Joan had a strong sense that something in the room was truly wrong—that there was an evil presence there.

As Joan prayed further she began to see a picture of a young child being beaten in that room. She knew that the Lord was showing her the reason that the evil presence lingered in Joey's room. Looking at Elaine, she said, "I believe that there may have been some kind of child abuse that took place in this room."

Stunned, Elaine began to explain to Joan that Joey's night terrors were often brought on by dreams of someone beating him. She had never understood this since neither she nor her husband had never struck him with that kind of force. "What can we do?" Elaine asked.

Grabbing Elaine's hand, Joan kneeled by the bed and began asking God to forgive the sin of child abuse that had taken place in that room. Tears came to their eyes as they identified with the young child who had suffered in this place. After a few minutes of dealing with these revelations and asking God to cleanse the room, Joan rose to her feet, and with authority in her voice, she commanded the evil presence to leave the property and never return. At that moment a great peace descended on the house. The room looked brighter. Elaine realized that for the first time since moving in, she felt totally at peace herself.

That night Joey slept well. Since praying through his room, the terror that plagued him never recurred. About a month after this incident, Elaine was visiting with her next door neighbor, who had lived there for several years. She asked about the family who had lived there before. Her neighbor told Elaine that she often heard yelling coming from the house, and that on three separate occasions the police had to come break up the fights. Although the neighbor was not sure, she heard through the neighborhood grapevine that the son was removed from the home by the authorities due to abuse suffered at the hands of his parents!

The Issues of Land and Property

Up to this point we have discussed the objects we own; but part of ridding our home of spiritual darkness has to do with the land on which we live as well. In this story of Elaine, we see that her young son was tormented by spiritual darkness that was not related to any object, or even any sin in which Elaine had been involved. The land on which they lived, however, had been defiled through sin, and that sin left an opening for demonic invasion that, until it was dealt with through prayer, continued to torment.

How can this be? Just as dark forces can inhabit an object, they can also inhabit land or places. In fact, some high ranking principalities and powers can inhabit whole cities or territories. But if the earth is the Lord's (Psalm 24:1), where do demons get the right to stake a claim to a particular part of the earth? The answer is through sin. Sin has a direct effect on land. We see that evidenced numerous times throughout the Bible.

In the story of Cain and Abel, for instance, remember that God said to Cain, "What have you done? The voice of your brother's blood cries out to Me from the ground. So now you are cursed from the earth, which has opened its mouth to receive your brother's blood from your hand" (Gen. 4:10,11). Sin produces a curse in the land—in the physical ground where it occurs—and where there are curses, evil abounds.

How Evil Gains a Foothold

The word "foothold" means a secure position that is a basis for further progress or development. When the enemy gains a foothold, he has firmly established himself in a position from which he can progress with his evil schemes to steal, kill, and destroy. Ephesians 4:25-27 says, "Therefore, putting away lying, 'Let each one of you speak truth with his neighbor,' for we are members of one another. 'Be angry, and do not sin': do not let the sun go down on your wrath, nor give place to the devil."

First, we must understand how Satan can gain a foothold in our own lives. If we allow sin into our lives and do not confess that sin, we leave a door open to give the enemy an opportunity to attack us and what is ours. This verse in Ephesians talks about anger. Even though anger is an emotion and can be righteous, we see here that if we do not operate in a godly manner when we are angry, it can embed in our emotions and open the door to the enemy to gain a foothold. The same is true of any sin that has not been cleansed by the blood of Jesus. Sin that has not been dealt with gives Satan a legal right into a situation, even into the life of a believer.

A great doctrinal debate through the history of Christendom has been the issue of demonic influence in the lives of true, born again believers. Most theologians do not have a problem with the concept of Satan's right to tempt a Christian. But if he could not gain some benefit into the lives of believers through that sin, why would he bother? Anyone with experience in the field of deliverance knows that Christians are prime targets for demonization, or a demonic foothold, within their lives. This does not mean that the person is "demon possessed," which is full control by a demonic entity, but rather that they are demonically influenced or tormented in a particular area of life. And the opening for demonization is often sin—either personal or generational.[1]

Just as the enemy can gain a foothold in our lives through sin, he can also gain a foothold into land through sin that has been committed there. Back to the verse in Ephesians, the phrase, "do not give place to the devil" means do not give him a foothold or opportunity. The Greek word for place in this verse is *topos*, from which we get the word topographical. It means a literal place, locality, or piece of land. Sin gives the enemy a foothold (secure position that is a basis of further progress or development) to *topos* (a literal place, locality, or piece of land). From that physical place where he has a foothold, he seeks to do his three favorite things: steal, kill, and destroy.

Therefore, the issue with our homes is not just what we own, but what has happened in our homes or on the land where it was built. Has any sin occurred that gives the enemy a place there? Remember the woman in the last chapter whose hair stood up on her arms? She was discerning a problem on the land. She had found evidence of occult rituals having been performed there. The land was undoubtedly full of demonic forces who had gained a foothold as a result of the ungodly worship. No wonder her hair stood up!

Sins That Defile Land

While any sin can be an opening for demonic activity, there are certain sins that can defile (bring a foul, dirty, uncleanness) in the land. These sins leave the land cursed and particularly susceptible to demonic footholds. They are:

1. Idolatry. As we discussed in Chapter Three, God hates idolatry. Just as the worship of God brings blessing upon the land, the worship of false gods brings curses.

2. Bloodshed. Earlier we mentioned the story of Cain and Abel. From this story we see that bloodshed affects the very land on which the violence occurred. As the blood of violence penetrates the ground, the Prince of the Power of the Air gains access to the land through the cursing caused by violence and bloodshed.

3. Immorality. This issue is one that we here in America must take seriously. Immorality has become a vague term, and a non-issue for those in power. Our society has come to believe that anyone can do whatever is right in their own sight. But Satan knows that every immoral act opens up a greater legal right for him to infiltrate land and homes. With the advent of the internet, there is even greater access to things like pornography and adult chat rooms. None of these things is benign. What is done in secret can bring serious consequences through defilement—not only of those involved, but of the land on which their sin occurred.

4. Covenant breaking. During the reign of King David, a great famine came on the land. When David inquired of the Lord concerning this famine, God said to him, "It is because of Saul and his bloodthirsty house, because he killed the Gibeonites" (2 Sam 21:1). The Gibeonites were a group of people who had entered into covenant with Israel in the days of Joshua. This covenant guaranteed their safety. Yet Saul broke covenant with the Gibeonites by murdering many of them and planning for the massacre of the rest. As a result, famine came on the land as God removed His blessing and Satan was allowed access. The famine did not strike immediately, but came when the new king came to power. Many of our homes in the United States have been built on land which was taken through broken treaties with Native Americans. Those broken treaties from years ago can defile and give the enemy a foothold in the land where we live today!

"But I Didn't Do the Sinning!"

You may be wondering why demonic forces in a place can torment a Christian if the Christian did not commit the sin that gave those forces the legal right to establish the foothold. This is where we must understand the spiritual principle of remitting sin. Hebrews 9:22 says, "And according to the law almost all things are purified with blood, and without shedding of blood there is no remission [of sin]."

The principle is this: No sin is atoned for without the shedding of blood. It was a principle in the Old Testament, it was a principle in the New Testament, and it is still a principle today. The difference between the Old and New Testament is Jesus. The blood that He shed on the cross is what we can appropriate to remit or atone for sin. But we must *appropriate* it in order for the sin to be remitted. Until repentance has occurred, and the blood of Jesus is applied, the sin—and thus, Satan's legal right to a foothold—remains intact.

Land that has been defiled through sin is like a soul that has been defiled through sin. Without repentance and the appropriation of the blood of Jesus, it remains defiled and Satan has a right to be there. A Christian taking control of a piece of property is *not* enough to rid it of spiritual darkness! Any demonic forces that had a foothold in that place will continue to operate from that foothold until they are expelled through the remitting of whatever sin gave them their right in the first place.

Finding Out What Needs Prayer

First, we must know what to pray for. The very first step is, of course, to repent of any known sin in which you or anyone else has participated in your home or on your land. Beyond that, there are two ways of figuring out what needs prayer: spiritual discernment and research. We already discussed spiritual discernment in the last chapter. There are many instances when you will not know the history of a place and must rely on the Lord to show you how to pray. One important question to ask while praying is, what is the fruit of the problem? Joey, for instance, was tormented by dreams of child abuse. That was a major clue. The fruit is connected to the root. Allow the Lord to fill in the blanks.

The other way of knowing what needs prayer is to be as familiar as possible with the history of the home or property. Go back as far as you can. Who originally owned the land? Was it part of a broken treaty with American Indians? Who has owned it since, and what has been their reputations? Has any illegal activity ever been recorded there? A trip to your local library and talking to a few neighbors can often reveal some very pertinent information. Remember, it does not matter if you own a home, or if you are renting an apartment. If you have a legal right to inhabit a place, then you have the spiritual authority to pray cleansing there.

Praying Over Land

When you get an idea about any sins that may have given the enemy a foothold in your home, the first step is to pray a prayer of repentance, like Joan did. Even though you may not have been the one that committed the sin, you can go to God on behalf of whoever committed the sin and ask forgiveness for that sin, applying the blood of Jesus to the land. This is called "identificational repentance."

Doing this does not mean that the person who actually committed the sin will not have to answer to God for his or her actions. They will. What identificational repentance does, however, is bring the blood of Jesus into the situation in order to cut off the ongoing effects of that sin. It shuts the door to demonic occupancy in that place. Any demonic forces that have been there because of a particular sin issue can, at that point, be commanded to leave in Jesus' Name, and they must do so because their legal right (which was linked with unremitted sin) has been removed. We can then pray and invite the Holy Spirit into the land and dedicate it for God's use. By doing these things, we actually have the power to bring cleansing to land that has been defiled and rid our homes of spiritual darkness.

A Word About Hotel Rooms

An interesting side note to the discussion of defiled land is hotel rooms. A great deal of immorality and who knows what else takes place in hotels—many times in the very rooms in which we stay and on the beds in which we sleep. Many good Christians have been inadvertently exposed to pornography through the television or through magazines left by others. Such things can hook otherwise innocent people into a lasting sin problem. So, how can we protect ourselves from a cheap shot by the enemy when we're on the road?

Because we have rented that room for a period of time, we

have legal spiritual authority over the atmosphere while we are there. A simple prayer can expel the demons and keep them from attacking us while we occupy that room. Whenever you get into a hotel room, stop and pray, asking God to forgive any sins of abuse, idolatry, bloodshed, immorality, covenant breaking, occult activity, or whatever else may be impressing you at the time. Then pray a prayer binding any forces linked with those sins from operating while you are there.

Also, pay special attention to the artwork and pictures. If anything looks strange, unnatural, or demonic, pray cleansing from evil spirits and pray that any curses attached to those objects would be broken. Taking the time to pray this way can make a tremendous difference in your trip!

Notes

[1] Other entry points for demonic forces include victimization, rejection, trauma, witchcraft, occult, fraternal orders (including Freemasonry), and cursing. An excellent study on this topic as it relates to land is Bob Beckett's *Commitment to Conquer* (Grand Rapids, MI: Chosen Books, 1997).

CHAPTER SIX

OVERTHROWING
GENERATIONAL CURSES

With the day's business behind me, I decided to take a walk and explore New Orleans. As I ventured out of my hotel, I took in the sights of a place where the excitement never seemed to end. Crowds of visitors, tourists, and locals lined both sides of Bourbon Street as they streamed in and out of shops, bars, restaurants, and establishments that offered live sex shows. Small groups gathered around jazz bands, many dancing to the music being played. I heard an occasional roar of laughter, along with an argument in what sounded like French.

As I walked along taking in all this activity, I found myself stopping in front of one particular shop. In the window was a beautiful ceramic cat with riveting blue eyes. The noise of the street seemed to fade as my concentration turned to the cat. I seemed drawn to it. I decided to take a closer look. The shop was filled with oddities, many of which were used in voodoo rituals. I thought little of it as I picked up the ceramic cat and gave it a closer inspection. Even though it was quite expensive, I had to have it. This beautiful cat would look great by the fireplace...

Generational Influences

In Chapter Four I told the rest of the story of this ceramic cat. One day the Lord revealed to me that witchcraft was linked to the cat. After all, it was purchased in, of all places, a shop with voodoo items. I should have known better, but at that time I was ignorant of the principles outlined in this book. Even so, many Christians would have shied away from the shop based on the weird feel of the place alone. But I did not. I felt, in fact, drawn into the shop. Why? Because of generational influences in my bloodline.

Occult practices were not unusual in the generations of my family. I had seen occult power at work. I remember one instance in particular when, as I was working with my grandfather one day, we encountered a wasps' nest in the middle of a doorway we were trying to get through. He looked at his palm, spoke something to it, held it up, and every one of the wasps dropped dead right before our eyes. He had used occult power to kill the wasps!

So, how is it that the actions of my grandfather and others in my ancestry had anything to do with my going into a questionable shop years later? It is because there was an inherited weakness toward sins of occult and witchcraft that had been passed down through my family's bloodline. That weakness, known as an iniquity, was operating in my life when I visited New Orleans and bought the cat. How can this be? Exodus 20:5 offers the answer: "For I, the LORD your God, am a jealous God, visiting the iniquity of the fathers on the children to the third and fourth generations." Sin not only affects the land, as we showed in the last chapter, it affects bloodlines for generations.

In her book *The Voice of God*, Cindy Jacobs helps us understand sin and iniquity as it relates to the generations: "The Bible speaks of them as two different things. Sin is basically the cause, and iniquity includes the effect. Generational iniquity works like this: A parent can commit a sin such as occultic involvement or sexual sin and that produces a curse. The curse then causes a generational iniquity or weakness to pass down in the family line.

Here is an example that might clarify this process. A pregnant woman is X-rayed and the unborn child becomes deformed by the X ray. The unborn child didn't order the X ray and is entirely a victim but, nonetheless, is affected by the X ray. Sin, like the X ray, damages the generations. This is an awesome thought and should put the fear of the Lord in us before we enter into sin."[1]

Iniquitous Patterns

Have you ever noticed how such things as alcoholism, divorce, laziness, or greed tend to run in families? These aren't just learned behaviors. They are manifestations of iniquity that have been passed down in the generations, or iniquitous patterns. Of course there are isolated instances of sin that seem to have nothing to do with previous generations. In that case, a new iniquitous pattern may be beginning in a family if that sin is not made right before God. But if you start looking around you with this in mind, you may be surprised at how many iniquitous patterns of sin you can find in family lines.[2]

Familial Spirits

Through the sin and iniquitous pattern, a familial spirit controls a certain person in a family. Sin is an opening for demonic forces to work in subsequent generations of a family through the iniquity produced. They know the family weaknesses and, therefore, entice, tempt, or lure family members with that weakness into the same or related sin. Spirits that are assigned to a family are called familial spirits. Some have been in families for generations on end.[3]

Generational Curses

The dictionary definition of a curse is the cause of evil, misfortune, or trouble. John Eckhardt of Crusaders Ministries defines it this way: "A curse is God's recompense in the life of a person and his or her descendants as a result of iniquity. The curse causes sorrow of heart and gives demonic spirits legal entry into a family whereby they can carry out and perpetuate their wicked devices."[4]

Eckhardt goes on to quote Derek Prince's seven common indications of a curse, which are chronic financial problems, chronic sickness and disease, female problems (I would add barrenness, whether brought on by the husband or the wife), accident prone, marital problems, premature death, and mental illness. Eckhardt adds mistreatment and abuse by others, and wandering or vagabond tendencies to the list.[5]

Such curses are produced because of the law of reaping and sowing. When that sin takes hold in the generations, a family curse is part of the effects of that sin.[6]

Looking For Generational Sin and Iniquity

There are certain things we can see in our family history that help us identify what problems may be affecting us today. In her book *The Voice of God*, Cindy Jacobs identifies four things that make us particularly susceptible to generational sin and iniquity.[7] They are:

1. Occultic involvement and witchcraft. Anything that draws its power from a source other than God is demonic in nature and can produce problems in the generations.

2. Secret societies, including Freemasonry, Eastern Star, and the Shriners. Members are often required to take oaths that actually curse themselves and their families.[8] If you or an ancestor has been involved in Freemasonry, please see Appendix Two of this book.

3. Robbing and defrauding God. If you withhold your tithe (10%) from God, the Bible says that you are actually robbing Him and that a curse can come into your household as a result (see Mal. 3:8,9). This curse often manifests as financial trouble, including poverty, and can be passed from generation to generation.

4. Bondages. Bondages are often passed down through family lines. Dean Sherman gives this definition of bondages: "If we continue in a habit of sin, we can develop a bondage. A bondage means that there is a supernatural element to our problem. The enemy now has a grip on a function of our personality."[9]

Back to the Cat

So, what do these generational influences have to do with ridding our homes of spiritual darkness? As we discussed in Chapter Three, objects that we own can often represent demonic strongholds in our lives. They can also represent iniquitous patterns, or generational curses, and may be the hiding place for familial spirits. That was the case with my ceramic cat. It represented a weakness in my family of being drawn to things linked with the occult (as we explained in Chapter Three, ceramic cats in general are not linked with demonic forces, but this particular one was). Ask the Lord to begin to show you what generational iniquities run in your family, and what objects you own that might be linked with those iniquities.

What About Heirlooms?

Does everything passed down to you from a grandparent have to go? Of course not! The issue is determining what items are

linked with iniquitous patterns, generational curses, or ungod-
liness, and removing those objects from your home. It may be
helpful to review the list of suspect objects in Chapter Three.

Getting rid of something you have purchased is one thing,
but destroying something that has been passed on to you may
be another matter. Many people are often unwilling to give up
something that may have belonged to an ancestor either out of
a sense of sentimentality, family pride, or a need to honor the
ancestor, which is especially prevalent in Asian cultures where
spiritism is a common practice.

Spiritism is communicating with demonic forces that are
linked with the dead. Spiritualism is the belief that the dead
survive as spirits that can communicate with the living. Many
people hold on to an object because they feel it links them with
someone who has died. In that case the object has become
more than a memento of a loved one. It has become a means
of keeping spiritual contact with the dead person. In reality,
the heirloom is not maintaining a link to their dead loved one,
but rather to a familial spirit who enjoys access to their homes
through deception.

We must ask ourselves what dark forces we may be allowing into our homes by owning certain heirlooms. Do those
objects honor God? Do they keep us in bondage to a generational curse or familial spirit? Can we reach the destiny God
has for us while continuing to allow openings to the demonic
in our own homes? And what effect do those objects have on
our children? Do we have a greater responsibility to honor
past generations or to mold new ones? Some things may be
difficult to let go of, but we must honestly measure what we
own against these kinds of questions, not only in our own minds,
but prayerfully before God.

If you remain unconvinced or have further questions about
the cause and effect of generational sin and iniquity, you may
want to read our book *Possessing Your Inheritance* (Renew

Books), which offers an in-depth treatment of the subject.

Notes

1 Cindy Jacobs, *The Voice of God*, (Ventura, CA: Regal Books, 1995), p. 64.

2 Taken from Chuck D. Pierce and Rebecca Wagner Sytsema, *Possessing Your Inheritance* (Ventura, CA: Renew Books), pp. 172-173.

3 Ibid., p. 174

4 John Eckhardt, *Identifying and Breaking Curses,* (Chicago, IL: Crusaders Ministries, 1995) p.1.

5 Ibid. p. 10

6 Pierce and Sytsema, pp. 175-176.

7 Cindy Jacobs, *The Voice of God*, (Ventura, CA: Regal Books, 1995), pp. 65-67.

8 For further study on Freemasonry, we recommend reading Chapter 10 of Noel and Phyl Gibson's *Evicting Demonic Intruders*, (Ventura, CA: Renew Books, 1993).

9 Dean Sherman, *Spiritual Warfare for Every Christian*, (Seattle, WA: Frontline Communications, 1990), p. 107.

CHAPTER SEVEN

PROTECTING OUR CHILDREN FROM SPIRITUAL DARKNESS

He who fears the LORD has a secure fortress, and for his children it will be a refuge.
(Prov. 14:26, NIV)

We have looked at many issues that allow spiritual darkness into a home. The goal of this chapter is to help parents understand some issues that are specific to their children. Securing your children's spiritual freedom is an important step to ridding your home of spiritual darkness.

The Importance of Order

Now that we have briefly discussed generational sin, let's look at God's order in the family, primarily focusing on children.

In Larry Christenson's book *The Christian Family*, he says, "The secret of good family life is disarmingly simple: *cultivate the family's relationship with Jesus Christ.* There is no phase of family life left outside this relationship. There is no problem a family might face which does not find its solution within the scope of this objective."[1]   The most important way to cultivate your family's relationship with the Lord is to establish God's divine order in your home.   God's divine order has to do with relationship and authority.

In both the Old and New Testaments, we find one key statement for children's relationships, and that is to obey their parents, for this is pleasing to the Lord and will create long life for them (see Col. 3:20 and Ex. 20).   A child's relationship to the Father, Jesus, and the Holy Spirit usually thrives and prospers in direct proportion to their obedience in the home and to their parents. If you can teach your child obedience as prescribed in Hebrews 12, they will not only become a child filled with joy and freedom, but they will mature into adults filled with faith.

The word "order" means to command or give orders in sequence to produce a specific result.   Order also means the arrangement of position and rank resulting in the ultimate accomplishment so that peace occurs in one's person or environment.   The word, therefore, includes both relationship and authority—the very things we need to cultivate the family's relationship to Jesus Christ.   Order also brings boundaries.   I believe the real key for a child's life is to show them the boundaries that have been established for their prosperity.   Those boundaries include being aware that owning certain things could give place to the enemy, who longs to steal their peace and prosperity from an early age.   It is very important, therefore, that we teach children to remove anything that enters their boundaries that would cause their peace to be lost or their prosperity to dwindle.

God's purpose is for us to be whole.   The sooner we teach this to our children, the better off they will be.   I Thessalonians 5:23 says, "Now may the God of peace Himself sanctify you completely, and may your whole spirit, soul and body be preserved blameless at the coming of our Lord Jesus Christ."   I believe this should be every parent's goal for their child.

Revisiting Generational Issues

With the basis we established for generational issues in the last chapter, let's take another look at those issues in relationship to the order of a child's life. Because a generational iniquity can be passed from generation to generation to generation, as it says in Exodus, I believe it's important to look for the patterns of generational iniquity in a child's life.

We can do this by observing a child's outward actions and by observing the items they are drawn to. One key symptom is an addiction that a child may form at a early age. Sometimes their appetites are totally out of control. Sometimes they have behavioral extremes and compulsive patterns. Often parents have been totally delivered of generational curses after a similar pattern begins appearing in their children. For instance, a parent might be a deceitful person but, through the blood of Jesus and spiritual discipline, overcome the problem in their own life only to find that their child is still deceitful. Any time we overcome a generational iniquity, it weakens that iniquitous pattern in the bloodline. I believe sometimes we can do away with it, but sometimes it appears in a weakened form.

My wife Pam and I have five children. Pam and I both had difficult childhoods that were mixed with both good and evil inheritances from the generations. Even though we have broken many generational iniquities and curses in our own lives, I do not assume the patterns have been totally annihilated. We always watch our children for signs of recurring patterns of what we know existed in the generations before us.

This principle is all through the word of God. When Joshua, for instance, went in to the promised land, he defeated many, but not all, of the enemies. Some still remained in the land. Then we see David, four generations later, ridding the land of the Jebusites. We need to be aware of this principle in light of our children.

Lessons From the Children's Home

In the early '80s, Pam and I had the privilege of becoming the administrators of one of the larger children's homes in Texas. This home was for children from broken families. Many of the kids were on the verge of becoming juvenile delinquents because the order of their lives had become so disrupted through a dysfunctional family unit. We learned many valuable lessons concerning the restoration of a child's innocence which would result in their future being reestablished. I believe sharing some of these experiences throughout this chapter will help the reader to better detect demonic behavior in children.

One 13-year-old boy, whom we loved dearly and were responsible for, had real problems with pornography and sexual addiction. His problem went far beyond any normal sexual curiosity. We knew we had authority over the cottage he lived in, as well as when he came into our personal home. Therefore, we knew that God had given us authority and influence to restore the godly order of his life.

We set boundaries over this child. We explained the evils of pornography to him. Whenever he stayed within those boundaries he was fine. However, every time he got out from under our authority, he would fall into the same patterns of sin—gaining access to pornographic materials. Pam and I began to cry out to God for his deliverance. We needed to find the entry point in his life that gave this demonic force right to influence him and keep him bound with pornographic materials.

We eventually learned that he was conceived out of wedlock and was born into a perverted situation. The environment he lived in was fatherless, and the male figures that came into his life had only presented a perverse example of masculinity. These facts helped us pray for his deliverance with great success. He is now a young man with a family who remains delivered to this day. The point is that sometimes we need to see how the objects to which our children are drawn may be linked with iniquitous patterns in their bloodline.

When the Enemy Infiltrates Boundaries

As was the case with this boy, it is important that we know how demons enter so that we can gain authority over their eviction. Take, for example, the story about the woman with the spirit of infirmity that caused her back to be bent over. The Bible says she had been bound for 18 years. This means that prior to that, she had been free, and at some point Satan afflicted her. You can always look back to the time when there was freedom to see where the enemy gained access. If there never has been freedom, we have authority through Jesus to establish it now.

I believe that every generation should excel beyond the one before. I want my children to establish a greater glory within their boundaries than I have. However, I also know that the enemy wants to infiltrate their boundaries, and not only bring them into captivity, but cause the ground they have gained to be lost. Because this is the case, I always want to be protective of the order in my children's lives until they have fully established God's authority for themselves. So I always review my children's boundaries and the order of their lives by the following:

   1. The generational bloodline, as we have been discussing.

   2. Their own personal sin. Remember kids are kids— they are born sinful and with free will. I, of course, try to steer them away from sinning. But, whenever I see my children choosing to sin, I look for the consequences of that sin in their lives. I can then explain why they are suffering those consequences so that they can develop a hatred within them of that sin.

   3. I look for any power of occult that has an influence in my children's life. The word "occult" simply means hidden, and

I find that Satan tries to create deception in order to hide the truth of sin to a child. My job is to expose sin for what it is.

4. Roots of bitterness and unforgiveness. One of the children that Pam and I were responsible for in the children's home had tremendous potential. I believe every child has potential, but this one was unique. However, he had been getting straight Fs in school and had been truant for two months. He had big problems. The Lord often revealed to me what this boy had in his possession. Sometimes it was drugs, other times it was weapons. He was eventually caught at school with drugs, and when I told him of the punishment the authorities at school set for him, he rebelled violently.

The Lord showed me a root of hate and murder within him. He had been a part of a very good family that had fallen apart because of his dad's infidelity. The bitterness from the loss was very deeply rooted. I remember the night that the root of bitterness was finally dealt with. When that occurred he immediately accepted the Lord as his Savior and his life and countenance changed suddenly and dramatically. He brought many, many things to me that represented his past nature and the bitterness that had been in him.

Dealing With a Younger Child

When dealing with younger children, demonic forces often torment them through fear. In their excellent book, *A Manual for Children's Deliverance*, Frank and Ida Mae Hammond say, "Night troublers are common: fear of the dark, fear of being left alone, or fear 'something is going to get you.' We have found such fears rooted in television programs, terrifying experiences, abusive treatment, and in toys and objects in the child's bedroom."[2]

When a child exhibits fear of something in his or her room, trace the fear to the source. It could be as simple as a shadow cast by a stuffed animal. In this case, just eliminate the shadow by moving the toy. At other times, the fear could be the result of some hidden item which needs to be uncovered. Enlist the child's assistance. Spend time "talking out" their fears. Because they are more aware of what bothers them than we are, they can often pinpoint the item. Allow them to go through their toys, games, music, pictures, and books to show you what is bothering them.

Children cannot always determine the source of their problems, however, and that's where they need your help. Here is a list of some items to watch for:

1. Video games with occult or martial arts themes.
2. Posters or a picture with occult or frightening images.
3. Books with scary pictures inside or on the cover.
4. Books of an occult or questionable origin.
5. Toys or other items of a frightening or occult nature.[3]

Let me offer a word of caution: Many parents worry about children's imaginations. There is a difference between creative, God-given imagination and occult fantasies. I have seen many parents harm the development of their child's godly imagination and creativity by "throwing out the baby with the bath water." Do not become legalistic with your child. This only causes the creativity of God not to be manifest in the child. This can also result in a poverty mentality.

You can learn the difference by seeing how your child's imagination is affecting his or her behavior. Are they obsessed by their fantasies or are the fantasies rooted in violence or anger? Here is where we can all use some parental common sense. As you are dealing with your children, remember that the forming of a child's conscience is important. We want to instill moral character, but not religious legalism. I have found it best to present my children with the right choice, instead of forcing a choice upon them.

As for teaching a child about spiritual discernment, here

is some good advice from Graham and Shirley Powell: "Children can easily grasp the realities of spiritual conflict, and should be taught how they can do their part to keep themselves walking closely with Jesus. But it is imperative that these truths be shared in wisdom so that there is no ground given for fear of the enemy. The reality of Jesus being Lord and Satan being defeated must be imparted. Continually center their attention on the love, power, and glory of the Lord Jesus Christ. Let them grow up Christ-conscious."[4]

Extending Boundaries

As children become older and mature, parents have to extend their boundaries. Every time you extend boundaries, you have to allow the child to establish new authority and responsibility within their new boundaries. You, therefore, have to watch for what new influences come into their lives. This can be very difficult for parents who would like their children to remain innocent and not train them to discern the evils they will encounter.

Music is a great example. One of our sons went to the movie Godzilla and used his own money to buy the soundtrack. About a week later, I just happened to be talking to him about the movie (which I would not have gone to see to start with) as he was playing the soundtrack. I heard a song that I thought was terrible and I tried to approach him to discuss the song and look at the words together. He resisted, so I just asked the Lord to show him. A few nights later he was visited by an evil, tangible presence. The force was the same color as that on the soundtrack cover. Because of the color, he knew that the evil presence was linked with the soundtrack he had bought. He immediately confessed the sin to me and his mother, destroyed the CD, and the evil presence left. Even though he still experiments with some music, he now understands that there can be evil power in it and exercises a level of discernment he did not previously have.

Hidden Things Revealed

As a child grows older, he or she may become involved in activities that they choose to hide from their parents. The Holy Spirit, however, has the power to reveal hidden things to parents. This was another lesson I learned while working at the Boys' Home. There was one particular boy who reminded me of Eddie Hascal on "Leave It To Beaver." He could be sweet, but he had a manipulative side we had to watch.

Once a month, these boys had the choice to go back and visit the homes they came from. These visits often caused a lot of problems, because the boys left the influence of a godly environment and were immersed in situations that caused their trouble in the first place. One weekend, our "Eddie Hascal" decided to go home. Pam and I went to church that Sunday as usual. During the service, there was an altar call. When I went up to the altar, the Lord began to reveal to me that "Eddie" was coming back with a duffel bag. The Lord also showed me everything that was inside this bag.

When he returned that afternoon, I explained to him what the Lord showed me at the altar. I then listed everything that was in his duffel bag, including rock music, snuff, and marijuana. "Eddie" turned white as a sheet. I was right on every count. He quickly repented and, more importantly, he saw the power of God to reveal the unknown. The Holy Spirit can reveal hidden things that could be causing danger to your kids. This is sometimes necessary when raising children.

Finally. . .

It is important that we as parents have a heart to see our children's wholeness. We must help them understand the order that God has established for their lives. We must make them aware that God wants them to prosper within the boundaries He has established for them. And finally, we must show them how to detect for themselves when anything detrimental enters or disrupts God's order in their lives. Trust God daily to rid your children's lives of spiritual darkness.

Notes

[1] Larry Christenson, *The Christian Family*, (Minneapolis, MN: Bethany House Publishing, 1970), p. 15.

[2] Frank and Ida Mae Hammond, *A Manual for Children's Deliverance*, (Kirkwood, MO: Impact Christian Books, Inc., 1996) p. 81.

[3] For a more complete list of games and toys to watch for, see *A Manual for Children's Deliverance*, listed above.

[4] Graham and Shirley Powell, *Christian Set Yourself Free*, (Kent, England: Sovereign World Ltd., 1983), p. 165.

CHAPTER EIGHT

TEN STEPS TO RIDDING YOUR HOME OF SPIRITUAL DARKNESS

Now that we have discussed a number of principles you need to know in order to do spiritual housecleaning, let's look at the whole process step-by-step. As you go through this chapter, please remember that this might take some time. Do not try to rush the process. For instance, you may find that you need more time to do personal repentance than you thought or to look through your house for offensive objects. Allow the Holy Spirit to set the pace for you.

Also, remember that you do not have to own your home or property to follow this list. If you rent a home or apartment, you have the spiritual right to evict Satan's cohorts.

Step One:
Accept Jesus as Your Lord and Savior

Most of the readers of this book have already taken this step, but for those of you who have not, the very first step to ridding your home of spiritual darkness is to secure your relationship with

God by accepting Jesus as your Lord and Savior. It is through Jesus' Name that we have the authority to expel demonic forces, and we cannot avail ourselves of His Name unless we have a relationship with Him.

But there is something much more important at stake, and that is your eternal home. Living with spiritual darkness on earth is one thing, but living in utter and complete darkness with no hope of life for all eternity is another. Only the blood of Jesus can save you from such an awful fate. If you have not already secured your salvation, please consider turning away from sin, believing in the death and resurrection of Jesus, and receiving Him as Lord and Savior of your life. To do this you must:

1. Consider your life and then turn away from everything that is contrary to what God wants (Matt. 3:7-10; Acts 3:19).

2. Acknowledge that Jesus Christ died on the Cross to forgive you of sin and that you take Him as your Savior to cleanse you from sin. Jesus paid the price due for your sin (Rom. 5:9,10; Titus 2:14).

3. Ask Him to be the Lord of your life, acknowledging openly and verbally that Jesus is not only your Savior, but your Lord (1 John 2:23).[1]

Step Two:
Take a Spiritual Inventory
of Your Life

In order to remove demonic forces from our homes and keep them out, we must be willing to deal with sin issues in our lives. As Charles Kraft, professor at Fuller Theological Seminary, would describe it, demons are like rats and sin is like garbage. "If we get rid of the rats and keep the garbage, the person is in great danger still. But if we get rid of the garbage, what we have done automatically affects the rats."[2] In other words, you must get rid of the garbage in order to get rid of the rats.

When we rid our lives of sin, demonic forces do not have the legal right they once had to occupy our lives and our homes. However, if we go through these steps to rid our homes of demonic forces without making our lives right before God, we may actually be making our situation worse!

Jesus taught that if we cast out a demon and it does not find rest elsewhere, the demon then comes back to check out the situation. If the demon finds the house is still suitable for occupation, then it goes and finds seven other demons who are even more wicked than itself and they all set up shop right back where they started. If we expel one demon, but do not remove its legal right, we get eight in return. "And the final condition of the man is worse than the first" (see Matt. 12:43-45).

Ask the Lord to reveal any sin issues in your life that must be dealt with before continuing in this process. Because unforgiveness is a big bag of garbage that demons love to feed on, ask God to show you any places of unforgiveness in your life toward others that need to be cleansed.

Step Three:
Dedicate Your Home
to the Lord

The next step in ridding your home of spiritual darkness is to dedicate your house to the Lord. Simply pray and invite the presence of the Lord into your home. Ask the Lord to use your home for His purposes. Declare that as for you and your house, you will serve the Lord (Josh. 24:15). Declare that your home will not be a haven for dark forces, but instead that it will be a beacon of light for your family and to the world. It is best to pray these things in an audible voice, which affirms your intentions not only to God and to yourself, but to any forces of darkness that are about to lose their dwelling place.

Step Four:
Prepare for Battle

What we are engaged in is spiritual warfare. We are warring in the heavenlies to establish our homes for the Lord and declare them off limits to the powers of darkness. Here are the preparations we should make as we go into battle:

1. Ask the Lord for the strategy for your war. He may lead you to play praise music throughout your home for a period of time, or He may lead you to read specific Scriptures in each room. Expect that He will answer your prayer and show you how to proceed.

2. Plead the blood of Jesus over yourself, your family, your animals, and your property.

3. Pray Psalm 91 out loud.

4. In Jesus' Name, bind any demonic forces from manifesting in your home during this process.

Step Five:
Take a Spiritual Inventory
of Your Home

Ask the Lord to give you the discernment you will need as you look at what you own. Go through your house, room by room, and let the Holy Spirit show you any objects that should not be in your home. Review the list of problem objects in Chapter Three. Examine your heirlooms as outlined in Chapter Six.

Step Six:
Cleanse Your Home
of Ungodly Objects

Whatever needs to go should not be considered an item for your next garage sale! Once you know something must go, be careful to destroy it. Deuteronomy 7:25 gives us an example to follow, "You shall burn the carved images of their gods with fire; you shall not covet the silver or gold that is on them, nor take it for yourselves, lest you be snared by it; for it is an abomination to the LORD your God."

Take what can be burned and burn it. If it cannot be burned, pass it through the fire (as a symbolic act of obedience) and then destroy it by whatever other means are available to you such as smashing or even flushing (I have known people to do this with jewelry that cannot be destroyed in other ways)!

Once you have destroyed the object, renounce any participation you or your family have had with that object (whether knowingly or unknowingly) and ask the Lord to forgive you. If the object is linked with Freemasonry, Eastern Star, Job's Daughters, Rainbow, or De Molay, pray the "Prayer of Release for Freemasons and Their Descendants" in the appendix of this book.

Because the legal right for demonic forces linked with that object has been removed through these acts, you can now command any demonic forces linked with that object to leave in the Name of Jesus.

Repeat these steps for every object that needs to go.

Step Seven:
Cleanse Each Room and
Cleanse the Land

Having cleansed your home of ungodly objects, the next step is to cleanse the spiritual atmosphere of each room. Demonic forces that were not attached to an object, but may be in the home because of sin or trauma which occurred there, need to be dealt with. Go through your house and repent for any known sin that has been committed in each room.

If your home was occupied by someone else before you, ask the Lord to show you what needs to be prayed in each room.

Trust the impressions you get during this process. Also, if you have noticed a major change in behavior or circumstances since moving into your home that cannot be explained any other way (e.g., fighting, financial troubles, violence, nightmares, accidents, etc.), this might be a clue as to what happened in your home before you moved in. Do identificational repentance in each room and over the land, as described in Chapter Five.

Pray that the Lord would heal any trauma caused by the torment of demonic forces in your home. For instance, in Chapter Five we told the story of three-year-old Joey who had been plagued with nightmares of child abuse. In a case like that, you should ask the Lord to touch Joey's mind with His healing balm so that he does not suffer lingering effects of the demonically induced nightmares.

Also, ask the Lord to restore to you and your family whatever blessings were stolen by the enemy through demonic forces in your home.

Step Eight, Part One:
Consecrate Your Home

Once you have completed all these steps, then go through your house, room by room, and consecrate each one to the Lord. Speak specific blessings into each room. In the living room you may want to bless the time that your family spends together there and ask the Lord to strengthen those relationships. In each bedroom, bless the plans and purposes that God has for each one that occupies that room. In the bedroom of a married couple, bless the sexual relationship and the union between husband and wife. Bless the work that goes on in an office or den and declare that all work done there will be done as unto the Lord. Think of why each room was designed, and bless that purpose. You can even bless the cleansing that goes on in the bathroom and ask the Lord to use it as a reminder of the cleansing He has brought in your own life!

Many who consecrate their home room by room often use oil to anoint the doors, windows, and furnishings. Oil is used as a symbol of Jesus' blood—a reminder of both the cleansing and protecting power in His blood. If you feel so led, using oil is certainly appropriate for this type of praying.

Step Eight, Part Two: Consecrate Your Property

Take a moment to review Chapter Five. Once you have completed the process outlined in that chapter, you can consecrate the land to the Lord. One way of doing this is to walk the perimeters of your property declaring that the land is consecrated, or set apart, for the Lord. This physical act helps to establish spiritual perimeters.

Another popular way for consecrating land is to stake the land and raise a canopy of praise. This is done by taking wooden stakes and driving one stake in each corner of the property while praying for the Lord's blessing. Then from the center of the property raising an imaginary canopy of praise to God by worshiping Him, singing songs, and declaring Scriptures. Neither of these methods (whether used together or by themselves) is a magic formula, but rather a symbolic or "prophetic" act that declares to the Lord, to the powers of darkness, and to yourself that this property is set apart (consecrated) for the Lord.

I recently moved my family from Denton, Texas, to Colorado Springs, Colorado. When we were getting settled in, we had a housewarming/consecration party in our new home. Along with about 30 friends, we took four oak stakes (about 2 inches thick) and with a heavy black marker we wrote Scripture references on each stake, one on each side of each stake. We used Scriptures such as Psalm 91, Isaiah 54:2-3, Jeremiah 29:7, Luke 1:37, and Joshua 24:15. Teams of about four or five then went to each corner of the property, read the Scriptures listed on their stakes, prayed a prayer of blessing and consecration, and then drove their stake into the ground using sledgehammers. We then met back in the house and began raising a canopy of praise by worshiping the Lord together.

If you choose to drive stakes on your property, ask the Lord what Scriptures you should use to consecrate the property to Him. You may come up with a whole different list than I did. You don't necessarily need to throw a party either. Do whatever is right for you and your situation.[3]

You can be as creative as you want in finding ways to consecrate your property. I have had friends who had their homes built with Bibles placed in the concrete foundation as a symbol that Christ is the foundation of their lives and property.

Step Nine:
Fill Your Home With Glory

The next step is to fill your home with objects and activities that bring glory to God. Jack Hayford offers this list of practices that promote healthy, happy, holy homes:

1. Take Communion with your family at home. Be sure to include the children.

2. Sing at home, both alone and together. Let your home be filled with the song of the Lord.

3. Pray at home. Pray as a family. Make table prayer meaningful, even though it is brief. Scheduled times of prayer are great, but so is prayer that rises naturally, and it helps the kids enter in as genuine participants instead of being forced.

4. Testify about the good things God has done for you at home. Dinnertime is a great time to talk about what Jesus did to help you today.

5. Speak the Word in your house. Besides your own devotional Bible reading, how about standing in the center of your

living room periodically and reading a psalm aloud?

6. Keep your house bright. Cultivate a genuine mood of hope in your home. Refuse whatever influence (moodiness, sharp speech, unworthy music, activities, or videos) would extinguish the brightness of God's glory light in your home.[4]

Step Ten:
Maintain Spiritual Victory

Keep on your toes! The enemy would love to find new and creative ways of infiltrating your home with spiritual darkness. It is a good idea to periodically go through your home and check for any new objects that should not be in your home, or pray through any new sin issues that have come up. In addition, plan on consecrating the rooms of your house and walking the perimeters of your property at least once a year. You might want to pick a day (like Good Friday) that will remind you each year that the time has come to do a spiritual checkup and rededicate your house to the Lord.

May the Lord richly bless you as you seek to rid your home of spiritual darkness and live in the glory of His presence!

Notes

[1] Steps taken from: Pat Robertson, "Spiritual Answers to Hard Questions," *The Spirit-Filled Life Bible* (Nashville, TN: Thomas Nelson Publishers, 1991), p. 1997.

[2] Charles H. Kraft, *Defeating Dark Angels*, (Ann Arbor, MI: Servant Publications, 1992), p. 43.

[3] Bob Beckett has written about staking a whole community in his book *Commitment to Conquer* (Chosen Books), which is an excellent resource for further study.

[4] Jack Hayford, *Glory on Your House* (Grand Rapids, MI: Chosen Books, 1991), pp. 94-104.

RECOMMENDED READING

Beckett, Bob. *Commitment to Conquer*. Grand Rapids, MI: Chosen Books, 1997. 162 pp. Strategic level spiritual warfare from the perspective of a local church pastor. Offers excellent understanding of issues regarding land and property.*

Gibson, Noel and Phyl. *Deliver Our Children from the Evil One*. Ventura, CA: Renew Books, 1992. 255 pp. This book offers both preventative and therapeutic solutions that defend children against satanic attacks.*

_____. *Evicting Demonic Intruders*. Ventura, CA: Renew Books, 1993. 320 pp. Used by Doris M. Wagner, Deliverance Concentration Coordinator for Wagner Leadership Institute, as her main text for deliverance seminars, this book offers some of the best insight and advice for ministering freedom from demonic forces.*

Hammond, Frank D. and Ida Mae Hammond. *Pigs in the Parlor*. Kirkwood, MO: Impact Books, 1973. 153 pp. One of the standard books on deliverance which has been in print for over twenty five years and has been helpful to many as an introduction to and handbook for casting out demons.*

_____. *A Manual for Children's Deliverance*. Kirkwood, MO: Impact Books, 1996. 138 pp. A sequel to *Pigs in the Parlor*, designed to deal specifically with evil influences and deliverance methods for children.*

Horrobin, Peter, *Healing Through Deliverance I: The Biblical Basis*. Ventura, CA: Renew Books, 1991. 311 pp. This book offers a comprehensive assessment of the place of deliverance ministry in the life of the church.*

_____. *Healing Through Deliverance II: The Practical Ministry*. Renew Books, Ventura, CA, 1995. 319 pp. This companion volume to the above book provides important foundational material for ministering healing and deliverance.*

Jacobs, Cindy. *Possessing the Gates of the Enemy*. Tarrytown, NY: Chosen Books, 1991. 247 pp. This lives up to its sub-title, "A Training

Manual for Militant Intercession." It has a wealth of information on prayer found in no other source.*

Kraft, Charles H. *Defeating Dark Angels*. Ann Arbor, MI: Servant Publications, 1992. 243 pp. A thorough and practical manual on personal deliverance from demons by a Fuller Seminary professor who draws from wide experience.*

_____. *I Give You Authority*. Grand Rapids, MI: Chosen Books, 1998. 336 pp. This book shows how to properly exercise the authority we have been given through the Holy Spirit in order to transform our lives and be free from satanic oppression.*

MacNutt, Francis. *Deliverance from Evil Spirits*. Grand Rapids, MI: Chosen Books, 1995, 277 pp. A highly-recommended practical manual on casting out demons.*

Murphy, Ed. *The Handbook for Spiritual Warfare*. Nashville, TN: Thomas Nelson Publishers, 1992. 520 pp. The most exhaustive textbook on spiritual warfare available. Very strong on biblical material.*

Pierce, Chuck D. and Rebecca Wagner Sytsema. *Possessing Your Inheritance*. Ventura, CA: Renew Books, 1999. 220 pp. This book offers clear principles for Christian living that help the reader understand and possess their inheritance in the Lord. Includes an extensive chapter on generational sin and iniquity.*

Smith, Eddie. *Spiritual Housecleaning*. SpiriTruth Publishing Company, 7710-T Cherry Park Drive, Suite 224, Houston, TX 77095, 1997. 43 pp. Through several stories, this book helps give an understanding of what objects should not be in a Christian home.

Wagner, C. Peter. *Hard-Core Idolatry: Facing the Facts*. Colorado Springs, CO: Wagner Publications, 1999. 43 pp. This book helps us recognize and cleanse our lives of "hard-core" idolatry.*

Wagner, C. Peter. *Radical Holiness for Radical Living*. Colorado Springs, CO: Wagner Publications, 1998. 41 pp. This book offers excellent principles for living a truly holy life.*

White, Thomas B. *The Believer's Guide to Spiritual Warfare*. Ann Arbor. MI: Servant Publications, 1990. 172 pp. This book offers much excellent material on our personal preparation for spiritual warfare.*

*These titles are available through The Arsenal.
For ordering information call toll-free 1-888-563-5150 or 1-719-262-9922

Prayer of Release for Freemasons and Their Descendants

If you were once a member of a Masonic organization or are a descendant of some-one who was, we recommend that you pray through this prayer from your heart. Please don't be like the Masons who are given their obligations and oaths one line at a time and without prior knowledge of the requirements. Please read it through first so you know what is involved. It is best to pray this aloud with a Christian witness present. We suggest a brief pause following each paragraph to allow the Holy Spirit to show any related issues which may require attention.

A significant number of people also reported having experienced physical and spiritual healings as diverse as long-term headaches and epilepsy as the result of praying through this prayer. Christian counsellors and pastors in many countries have been using this prayer in counselling situations and seminars for several years, with real and significant results.

There are differences between British Commonwealth Masonry and Ameri-can & Prince Hall Masonry in the higher degrees. Degrees unique to Americans are marked with 3 stars at the beginning of each paragraph. Those of British & Common-wealth decent shouldn't need to pray through those paragraphs.

Father God, creator of heaven and earth, I come to you in the name of Jesus Christ your Son. I come as a sinner seeking forgiveness and cleansing from all sins commit-ted against you, and others made in your image. I honor my earthly father and mother and all of my ancestors of flesh and blood, and of the spirit by adoption and godpar-ents, but I utterly turn away from and renounce all their sins. I forgive all my ances-tors for the effects of their sins on me and my children. I confess and renounce all of my own sins. I renounce and rebuke Satan and every spiritual power of his affecting me and my family.

I renounce and forsake all involvement in Freemasonry or any other lodge or craft by my ancestors and myself. In the name of Jesus Christ, I renounce and cut off Witchcraft, the principal spirit behind Freemasonry, and I renounce and cut off Baphomet, the Spirit of Antichrist and the spirits of Death, and Deception. I renounce the insecurity, the love of position and power, the love of money, avarice or greed, and the pride which would have led my ancestors into Masonry. I renounce all the fears which held them in Masonry, especially the fears of death, fears of men, and fears of trusting, in the name of Jesus Christ.

I renounce every position held in the lodge by any of my ancestors or myself, including "Master," "Worshipful Master," or any other. I renounce the calling of any man "Master," for Jesus Christ is my only master and Lord, and He forbids anyone else having that title. I renounce the entrapping of others into Masonry, and observing the helplessness of others during the rituals. I renounce the effects of Masonry passed on to me through any female ancestor who felt distrusted and rejected by her husband as he entered and attended any lodge and refused to tell her of his secret activities. I also renounce all obligations, oaths and curses enacted by every female member of my family through any direct membership of all Women's Orders of Freemasonry, the Order of the Eastern Star, or any other Masonic or occultic organization.

33rd & Supreme Degree

In the name of Jesus Christ I renounce the oaths taken and the curses involved in the supreme Thirty-Third Degree of Freemasonry, the Grand Sovereign Inspector General. I renounce the secret passwords, DEMOLAY-HIRUM ABIFF, FREDERICK OF PRUSSIA, MICHA, MACHA, BEALIM, and ADONAI and all they mean. I renounce all of the obligations of every Masonic degree, and all penalties invoked. I renounce and utterly forsake The Great Architect Of The Universe, who is revealed in the this degree as Lucifer, and his false claim to be the universal fatherhood of God. I renounce the cable-tow around the neck. I renounce the death wish that the wine drunk from a human skull should turn to poison and the skeleton whose cold arms are invited if the oath of this degree is violated. I renounce the three infamous assassins of their grand master, law, property and religion, and the greed and witchcraft involved in the attempt to manipulate and control the rest of mankind. In the name of God the Father, Jesus Christ the Son, and the Holy Spirit, I renounce and break the curses involved in the idolatry, blasphemy, secrecy and deception of Freemasonry at every level, and I appropriate the Blood of Jesus Christ to cleanse all the consequences of these from my life. I now revoke all previous consent given by any of my ancestors or myself to be deceived.

Blue Lodge

In the name of Jesus Christ I renounce the oaths taken and the curses involved in the First or Entered Apprentice Degree, especially their effects on the throat and tongue. I renounce the Hoodwink blindfold and its effects on spirit, emotions and eyes, including all confusion, fear of the dark, fear of the light, and fear of sudden noises. I renounce the blinding of spiritual truth, the darkness of the soul, the false imagination, condescension and the spirit of poverty caused by the ritual of this degree. I also renounce the usurping of the marriage covenant by the removal of the wedding ring. I renounce the secret word, BOAZ, and all it means. I renounce the serpent clasp on the apron, and the spirit of Python which it brought to squeeze the spiritual life out of me. I renounce the ancient pagan teaching from Babylon & Egypt and the symbolism of the First Tracing Board. I renounce the mixing and mingling of truth and error, the mythology, fabrications and lies taught as truth, and the dishonesty by leaders as to the true understanding of the ritual, and the blasphemy of this degree of Freemasonry. I renounce the presentation to every compass direction, for all the Earth is the Lord's, and everything in it.

I renounce the cabletow noose around the neck, the fear of choking and also every spirit causing asthma, hayfever, emphysema or any other breathing difficulty. I renounce the ritual dagger, or the compass point, sword or spear held against the breast, the fear of death by stabbing pain, and the fear of heart attack from this degree, and the absolute secrecy demanded under a witchcraft oath and sealed by kissing the Volume of the Sacred Law. I also renounce kneeling to the false deity known as the Great

Architect of the Universe, and humbly ask the One True God to forgive me for this idolatry, in the name of Jesus Christ. I renounce the pride of proven character and good standing required prior to joining Freemasonry, and the resulting self-righteousness of being good enough to stand before God without the need of a saviour. I now pray for healing of... (throat, vocal cords, nasal passages, sinus, bronchial tubes etc.) for healing of the speech area, and the release of the Word of God to me and through me and my family.

In the name of Jesus Christ I renounce the oaths taken and the curses involved in the Second or Fellow Craft Degree of Masonry, especially the curses on the heart and chest. I renounce the secret words SHIBBOLETH and JACHIN, and all that these mean. I renounce the ancient pagan teaching and symbolism of the Second Tracing Board. I renounce the Sign of Reverence to the Generative Principle. I cut off emotional hardness, apathy, indifference, unbelief, and deep anger from me and my family. In the name of Jesus' Christ I pray for the healing of ...(the chest/lung/heart area) and also for the healing of my emotions, and ask to be made sensitive to the Holy Spirit of God.

In the name of Jesus Christ I renounce the oaths taken and the curses involved in the Third or Master Mason Degree, especially the curses on the stomach and womb area. I renounce the secret words TUBAL CAIN and MAHA BONE, and all that they mean. I renounce the ancient pagan teaching and symbolism of the Third Tracing Board used in the ritual. I renounce the Spirit of Death from the blows to the head enacted as ritual murder, the fear of death, false martyrdom, fear of violent gang attack, assault, or rape, and the helplessness of this degree. I renounce the falling into the coffin or stretcher involved in the ritual of murder. In the name of Jesus Christ I renounce Hiram Abiff, the false saviour of Freemasons revealed in this degree. I renounce the false resurrection of this degree, because only Jesus Christ is the Resurrection and the Life! In the name of Jesus Christ I pray for the healing of... (the stomach, gall bladder, womb, liver, and any other organs of my body affected by Masonry), and I ask for a release of compassion and understanding for me and my family.

I renounce the pagan ritual of the "Point within a Circle" with all its bondages and phallus worship. I renounce the symbol "G" and its veiled pagan symbolism and bondages. I renounce the occultic mysticism of the black and white mosaic checkered floor with the tessellated boarder and five-pointed blazing star.

I renounce the All-Seeing Third Eye of Freemasonry or Horus in the forehead and its pagan and occult symbolism. I now close that Third eye and all occult ability to see into the spiritual realm, in the name of the Lord Jesus Christ, and put my trust in the Holy Spirit sent by Jesus Christ for all I need to know on spiritual matters. I renounce all false communions taken, all mockery of the redemptive work of Jesus Christ on the cross of Calvary, all unbelief, confusion and depression. I renounce and forsake the lie of Freemasonry that man is not sinful, but merely imperfect, and so can redeem himself through good works. I rejoice that the Bible states that I cannot do a single thing to earn my salvation, but that I can only be saved by grace through faith in Jesus Christ and what He accomplished on the Cross of Calvary.

I renounce all fear of insanity, anguish, death wishes, suicide and death in the name of Jesus Christ. Death was conquered by Jesus Christ, and He alone holds the keys of death and hell, and I rejoice that He holds my life in His hands now. He came to give me life abundantly and eternally, and I believe His promises.

I renounce all anger, hatred, murderous thoughts, revenge, retaliation, spiritual apathy, false religion, all unbelief, especially unbelief in the Holy Bible as God's Word, and all compromise of God's Word. I renounce all spiritual searching into false religions, and all striving to please God. I rest in the knowledge that I have found my Lord and Saviour Jesus Christ, and that He has found me.

York Rite

I renounce and forsake the oaths taken and the curses involved in the York Rite Degrees of Masonry. I renounce the Mark Lodge, and the mark in the form of squares and angles which marks the person for life. I also reject the jewel or occult talisman which may have been made from this mark sign and worn at lodge meetings;

the Mark Master Degree with its secret word JOPPA, and its penalty of having the right ear smote off and the curse of permanent deafness, as well as the right hand being chopped off for being an imposter.

I also renounce and forsake the oaths taken and the curses involved in the other York Rite Degrees, including Past Master, with the penalty of having my tongue split from tip to root;

and of the Most Excellent Master Degree, in which the penalty is to have my breast torn open and my heart and vital organs removed and exposed to rot on the dung hill.

Holy Royal Arch Degree

In the name of Jesus Christ, I renounce and forsake the oaths taken and the curses involved in the Holy Royal Arch Degree especially the oath regarding the removal of the head from the body and the exposing of the brains to the hot sun. I renounce the false secret name of God, JAHBULON, and declare total rejection of all worship of the false pagan gods, Bul or Baal, and On or Osiris. I also renounce the password, AMMI RUHAMAH and all it means. I renounce the false communion or Eucharist taken in this degree, and all the mockery, scepticism and unbelief about the redemptive work of Jesus Christ on the cross of Calvary. I cut off all these curses and their effects on me and my family in the name of Jesus Christ, and I pray for... (healing of the brain, the mind etc.)

I renounce and forsake the oaths taken and the curses involved in the Royal Master Degree of the York Rite; the Select Master Degree with its penalty to have my hands chopped off to the stumps, to have my eyes plucked out from their sockets, and to have my body quartered and thrown among the rubbish of the Temple.

I renounce and forsake the oaths taken and the curses involved in the Super Excellent Master Degree along with the penalty of having my thumbs cut off, my eyes put out, my body bound in fetters and brass, and conveyed captive to a strange land; and also of the Knights Order of the Red Cross, along with the penalty of having my house torn down and my being hanged on the exposed timbers.

I renounce the Knights Templar Degree and the secret words of KEB RAIOTH, and also Knights of Malta Degree and the secret words MAHER-SHALAL-HASH-BAZ.

I renounce the vows taken on a human skull, the crossed swords, and the curse and death wish of Judas of having the head cut off and placed on top of a church spire. I renounce the unholy communion and especially of drinking from a human skull in many Rites.

Ancient & Accepted or Scottish Rite (only the 18th, 30th, 31st 32nd & 33rd degree are operated in British Commonwealth countries.)

*** I renounce the oaths taken and the curses and penalties involved in the American and Grand Orient Lodges, including of the Secret Master Degree, its secret password of ADONAI, and its penalties;

*** of the Perfect Master Degree, its secret password of MAH-HAH-BONE, and its penalty of being smitten to the Earth with a setting maul;

*** of the Intimate Secretary Degree, its secret password of JEHOVAH used blasphemously, and its penalties of having my body dissected, and of having my vital organs cut into pieces and thrown to the beasts of the field;

*** of the Provost and Judge Degree, its secret password of HIRUM-TITO-CIVI-KY, and the penalty of having my nose cut off;

*** of the Intendant of the Building Degree, of its secret password AKAR-JAI-JAH, and the penalty of having my eyes put out, my body cut in two and exposing my bowels;

*** of the Elected Knights of the Nine Degree, its secret password NEKAM NAKAH, and its penalty of having my head cut off and stuck on the highest pole in the East;

*** of the Illustrious Elect of Fifteen Degree, with its secret password ELIGNAM, and its penalties of having my body opened perpendicularly and horizontally, the entrails exposed to the air for eight hours so that flies may prey on them, and for my head to be cut off and placed on a high pinnacle;

*** of the Sublime Knights elect of the Twelve Degree, its secret password STOLKIN-ADONAI, and its penalty of having my hand cut in twain;

*** of the Grand Master Architect Degree, its secret password RAB-BANAIM, and its penalties;

*** of the Knight of the Ninth Arch of Solomon Degree, its secret password JEHOVAH, and its penalty of having my body given to the beasts of the forest as prey;

*** of the Grand Elect, Perfect and Sublime Mason Degree, its secret password, and its penalty of having my body cut open and my bowels given to vultures for food;

Council of Princes of Jerusalem

*** of the Knights of the East Degree, its secret password RAPH-O-DOM, and its penalties;

*** of the Prince of Jerusalem Degree, its secret password TEBET-ADAR, and its penalty of being stripped naked and having my heart pierced with a ritual dagger;

Chapter of the Rose Croix

*** of the Knight of the East and West Degree, its secret password ABADDON, and its penalty of incurring the severe wrath of the Almighty Creator of Heaven and Earth;

18th Degree

I renounce the oaths taken and the curses and penalties involved in the Eighteenth Degree of Masonry, the Most Wise Sovereign Knight of the Pelican and the Eagle and

Sovereign Prince Rose Croix of Heredom. I renounce and reject the Pelican witchcraft spirit, as well as the occultic influence of the Rosicrucians and the Kabbala in this degree.

I renounce the claim that the death of Jesus Christ was a "dire calamity," and also the deliberate mockery and twisting of the Christian doctrine of the Atonement. I renounce the blasphemy and rejection of the deity of Jesus Christ, and the secret words IGNE NATURA RENOVATUR INTEGRA and its burning. I renounce the mockery of the communion taken in this degree, including a biscuit, salt and white wine.

Council of Kadosh

*** I renounce the oaths taken and the curses and penalties involved in the Grand Pontiff Degree, its secret password EMMANUEL, and its penalties;

*** of the Grand Master of Symbolic Lodges Degree, its secret passwords JEKSON and STOLKIN, and the penalties;

*** of the Noachite of Prussian Knight Degree, its secret password PELEG, and its penalties;

*** of the Knight of the Royal Axe Degree, its secret password NOAH-BEZALEEL-SODONIAS, and its penalties;

*** of the Chief of the Tabernacle Degree, its secret password URIEL-JEHO-VAH, and its penalty that I agree the Earth should open up and engulf me up to my neck so I perish;

*** of the Prince of the Tabernacle Degree, and its penalty that I should be stoned to death and my body left above ground to rot;

*** of the Knight of the Brazen Serpent Degree, its secret password MOSES-JOHANNES, and its penalty that I have my heart eaten by venomous serpents;

*** of the Prince of Mercy Degree, its secret password GOMEL, JEHOVAH-JACHIN, and its penalty of condemnation and spite by the entire universe;

*** of the Knight Commander of the Temple Degree, its secret password SOLOMON, and its penalty of receiving the severest wrath of Almighty God inflicted upon me;

*** of the Knight Commander of the Sun, or Prince Adept Degree, its secret password STIBIUM, and its penalties of having my tongue thrust through with a red-hot iron, of my eyes being plucked out, of my senses of smelling and hearing being removed, of having my hands cut off and in that condition to be left for voracious animals to devour me, or executed by lightening from heaven;

*** of the Grand Scottish Knight of Saint Andrew Degree, its secret password NEKAMAH-FURLAC, and its penalties;

*** of the Council of Kadosh Grand Pontiff Degree, its secret password EMMANUEL, and its penalties;

I renounce the oaths taken and the curses involved in the Thirtieth Degree of Masonry, the Grand Knight Kadosh and Knight of the Black and White Eagle. I renounce the secret passwords, STIBIUM ALKABAR, PHARASH-KOH and all they mean.

Sublime Princes of the Royal Secret

I renounce the oaths taken and the curses involved in the Thirty-First Degree of Masonry, the Grand Inspector Inquisitor Commander. I renounce all the gods and goddesses of Egypt which are honored in this degree, including Anubis with the ram's head, Osiris the Sun god, Isis the sister and wife of Osiris and also the moon goddess. I renounce the Soul of Cheres, the false symbol of immortality, the Chamber of the dead and the false teaching of reincarnation.

I renounce the oaths taken and the curses involved in the Thirty-Second Degree of Masonry, the Sublime Prince of the Royal Secret. I renounce the secret passwords, PHAAL/PHARASH-KOL and all they mean. I renounce Masonry's false trinitarian deity AUM, and its parts; Brahma the creator, Vishnu the preserver and Shiva the destroyer. I renounce the deity of AHURA-MAZDA, the claimed spirit or source of all light, and the worship with fire, which is an abomination to God, and also the drinking from a human skull in many Rites.

Shriners (Applies only in North America)

*** I renounce the oaths taken and the curses and penalties involved in the Ancient Arabic Order of the Nobles of the Mystic Shrine. I renounce the piercing of the eyeballs with a three-edged blade, the flaying of the feet, the madness, and the worship of the false god Allah as the god of our fathers. I renounce the hoodwink, the mock hanging, the mock beheading, the mock drinking of the blood of the victim, the mock dog urinating on the initiate, and the offering of urine as a commemoration.

All other degrees

I renounce all the other oaths taken, the rituals of every other degree and the curses involved. These include the Allied Degrees, The Red Cross of Constantine, the Order of the Secret Monitor, and the Masonic Royal Order of Scotland. I renounce all other lodges and secret societies including Prince Hall Freemasonry, Grand Orient Lodges, Mormonism, The Order of Amaranth, the Royal Order of Jesters, the Manchester Unity Order of Oddfellows, Buffalos, Druids, Foresters, the Orange and Black Lodges, Elks, Moose and Eagles Lodges, the Ku Klux Klan, The Grange, the Woodmen of the World, Riders of the Red Robe, the Knights of Pythias, the Mystic Order of the Veiled Prophets of the Enchanted Realm, the women's Orders of the Eastern Star, of the Ladies Oriental Shrine, and of the White Shrine of Jerusalem, the girls' order of the Daughters of the Eastern Star, the International Orders of Job's Daughters, and of the Rainbow, and the boys' Order of De Molay, and their effects on me and all my family.

Lord Jesus, because you want me to be totally free from all occult bondages, I will burn all objects in my possession which connect me with all lodges and occultic organizations, including Masonry, Witchcraft and Mormonism, and all regalia, aprons, books of rituals, rings and other jewelry. I renounce the effects these or other objects of Masonry, including the compass and the square, have had on me or my family, in the name of Jesus Christ.

I renounce every evil spirit associated with Masonry and Witchcraft and all other sins, and I command in the name of Jesus Christ for Satan and every evil spirit to be bound and to leave me now, touching or harming no-one, and go to the place appointed for you by the Lord Jesus, never to return to me or my family. I call on the name of the Lord Jesus to be delivered of these spirits, in accordance with the many promises of the Bible. I ask to be delivered of every spirit of sickness, infirmity, curse, affliction, addiction, disease or allergy associated with these sins I have confessed and renounced. I surrender to God's Holy Spirit and to no other spirit all the places in my life where these sins have been.

(All participants should now be invited to sincerely carry out in faith the following actions):

(1) Symbolically remove the blindfold (hoodwink) and give it to the Lord for disposal;

(2) in the same way, symbolically remove the veil of mourning;

(3) Symbolically cut and remove the noose from around the neck, gather it up with the cabletow running down the body and give it all to the Lord for His disposal;

(4) Renounce the false Freemasonry marriage covenant, removing from the 4th finger of the right hand the ring of this false marriage covenant, giving it to the Lord to dispose of it;

(5) Symbolically remove the chains and bondages of Freemasonry from your body;

(6) symbolically remove all Freemasonry regalia and armor, especially the Apron;

(7) Invite participants to repent of and seek forgiveness for having walked on all unholy ground, including Freemasonry lodges and temples, including any Mormon or any other occultic/Masonic organizations.

(8) Symbolically remove the ball and chain from the ankles.

(9) Proclaim that Satan and his demons no longer have any legal rights to mislead and manipulate the person seeking help.)

Holy Spirit, I ask that you show me anything else which I need to do or to pray so that I and my family may be totally free from the consequences of the sins of Masonry, Witchcraft, Mormonism and all related Paganism and Occultism.

(Pause, while listening to God, and pray as the Holy Spirit leads you.)

Now, dear Father God, I ask humbly for the blood of Jesus Christ, your Son and my Saviour, to cleanse me from all these sins I have confessed and renounced, to cleanse my spirit, my soul, my mind, my emotions and every part of my body which has been affected by these sins, in the name of Jesus Christ. I also command every cell in my body to come into divine order now, and to be healed and made whole as they were designed to by my loving Creator, including restoring all chemical imbalances and neurological functions, controlling all cancerous cells, and reversing all degenerative diseases, in the name of the Lord Jesus Christ.

I ask you, Lord, to baptize me in your Holy Spirit now according to the promises in your Word. I take to myself the whole armor of God in accordance with Ephesians Chapter Six, and rejoice in its protection as Jesus surrounds me and fills me with His Holy Spirit. I enthrone you, Lord Jesus, in my heart, for you are my Lord and my Saviour, the source of eternal life. Thank you, Father God, for your mercy, your forgiveness and your love, in the name of Jesus Christ, Amen.

Since the above is what needs to be renounced, why would anyone want to join? Copying of this prayer is both permitted and encouraged provided reference is made to where it comes from. Written testimonies of changed lives and healings are welcome. Additions to this prayer will be added to our Internet site was well as for other lodges or secret or occultic organizations. These may be freely downloaded for wider use. If additional prayer and ministry is required following the above prayer, please contact the Jubilee Essential Resources who may refer you to someone closer to you.

We have competent counsellors in most countries around the world.

With the exception of using Americanized spelling, this prayer is taken from the website **www.jubilee.org.nz**, published by Jubilee Publishers. We are very grateful to Selwyn Stevens for compiling this prayer and for making it available to all who need it.

For further information on Freemasonry, please contact:

Jubilee Ministries Trust Incorporated
PO Box 36-044
Wellington 6330
New Zealand
Phone/Fax 64-4-568-4533